EVERYWHERE

"Elsewhere: Everywhere"
Various
First Published 2012

Published by Cargo Publishing & McSweeney's
978-1-908885-08-1

Bic Code-FA Modern & Contemporary Fiction
FYB Short Stories

Published in association with the Edinburgh International Book Festival,
with the support of Creative Scotland and the Scottish Government's
Edinburgh Festivals Expo Fund.

Also available as:
Ebook
Kindle ebook

Printed & bound in China by Shanghai Offset Printing Products Ltd.
Cover illustrations by Jack Teagle
Designed by McSweeney's

www.cargopublishing.com
www.mcsweeneys.net
www.edbookfest.co.uk
www.jackteagle.co.uk

PAPER BOAT,
PAPER BIRD

by DAVID ALMOND

KYOTO. KY-O-TO! KYO-TO! She feels so weirdly at home. She is herself, Mina, but it's like there's another Mina waiting to be discovered or created here.

'That's travel,' says her mum. 'Turns the world into somewhere else and turns you into someone else.'

This morning they're off to the Golden Temple. They're on a packed bus. Mina stands squashed in the aisle. Her mum's at the front, watching for the temple stop. She keeps turning and peering through the bodies. Mina waves: don't worry. Look! Here I am!

There's a woman sitting on a seat beside her. The woman appears to be completely on her own. She's calmly folding a square sheet of paper. She folds it edge to edge, point to point. She opens it, closes it, tugs and teases it into shape. Her lips move, as if she's silently singing in time with the movement of her fingers. She swiftly makes a little boat. She holds it on her open palm and moves her hand gently back and forward, up and down. It's like she's on the bus but not on the bus. The boat moves as if it's floating on a lake inside the bus that's there for anyone to know.

She sees Mina watching. She smiles and bows her head.

'Konichiwa,' she says.

Mina smiles and bows her head as well.

'Konichiwa.'

She feels the strange neat movements of her lips and throat and tongue as they make the lovely word. She says it again to feel the word in her mouth and to hear the sharp sound of it.

'Ko-ni-chi-wa.'

The woman floats the boat towards Mina with her hands.

Go on, take it, she says with her eyes.

Mina takes it and rests it on her own palm.

'Arigato,' she says. 'A-ri-ga-to.'

Float it, says the woman with her eyes.

Mina floats it through the tiny empty spaces around her body and the spaces open and the waters rise.

The woman laughs and claps her hands silently. She starts on another sheet of paper – folds it, creases it, tugs and teases it into shape. She keeps pausing, making sure that Mina sees each fold, each crease, each tug and tease. Look, she's saying, this is how it's done. Mina watches the woman's fingers and the crowds around her disappear. Kyoto is gone. The bus is gone. She imagines what it would be like to be a sheet of paper in the woman's hands, to be folded and creased and teased into shape, to become a paper Mina.

Maybe the woman knows this. She smiles deep into Mina's eyes as if she knows everything.

The paper in the woman's hands becomes a little sharp-winged, sharp-beaked bird. She holds it between her thumb and fingers and flies it through the spaces around her. She flies it towards Mina.

Take it, she says with her eyes. Fly it.

'Arigato,' says Mina.

She takes the bird. She can feel the vibrations of the woman's fingers within it. With the bird flying between her fingers, she's surrounded by empty air, by great stretches of water.

The bus sighs to a halt. The woman shrugs, smiles, stands up.

'Sayonara,' she says.

She hands Mina some sheets of paper.

'Sa-yo-na-ra,' says Mina. 'A-ri-ga-to.'

The woman twists her way to the opening door and she steps out into the crowds.

Mina looks through her own reflection into the street outside. She sees the woman then loses sight of her then sees her again but the crowds close around her and the bus moves on and she's gone.

Mina carefully folds the boat and the bird flat and puts them into her sketchbook with the sheets of paper.

The bus continues through the busy streets, through all the noise, past skyscrapers, hotels, flower sellers, flashing lights, cyclists, geishas, sushi shops, punks, cinemas, statues, tourist groups, burger bars, lanterns, pachinko parlours, shrines, road signs, lorries, buses, cars, crowds.

Mina sees how beautiful it all is. So much of it is recognisable, but so much of it is just so strange. The bus glides and sways. The bodies around her sway against her. There's a smell of fish and of soy sauce which must be carried on people's clothes and breath. The thrill of being here in Kyoto! She remembers roaring up into the clouds and leaving England behind. Then the oceans they crossed, the sky they flew through, the mountains and countries and cities below. Now home is on the earth's far side and this is Japan. She saw it first at the crack of dawn from miles up in the sky. There it was, the country that seemed to float on the sea.

'Ja-pan,' she whispers. 'Ky-o-to!'

She feels the little bursts of breath in her mouth. She thinks of the world turning and turning through endless space. She feels the great stretches of emptiness that are inside her.

'Mina!' calls her mum. 'Mina, here we are!'

The bodies part, letting Mina through.

'Here I am,' she says.

They walk along the path towards the temple gardens.

'Keep close,' says her mum. 'Don't get lost.'

Mina shows her lovely paper gifts.

She floats the boat and flies the bird.

They buy their tickets, which bear the name of the place then a picture of it, then unreadable and beautiful writing beneath.

The gravel gently rattles under their feet as they walk through the gates. There are rocks, pine trees, narrow pathways, stone lanterns, then the lake, then the golden temple, and beyond the temple there are trees, low hills then dark and distant mountains and the sky.

'The temple's called Kinkaku-ji,' says her mum.

'Kin-ka-ku-ji,' says Mina.

'It contains the ashes of Buddha. It was burned down by a distressed monk in 1950 and was rebuilt again. It is considered to be the same place, even though it's new.'

She sighs and laughs at the outrageous idea, at the outrageous beauty of the place.

'Maybe it suggests that nothing is ever truly lost, that everything will return.'

'Maybe,' says Mina.

She thinks of her lost dad for a few moments, as she does each day. He would have loved this place so much. Then she turns her mind back to the temple.

It is reflected in the lake. It appears to be floating on another temple. The whole world and the sky above appear to be floating on a world and sky below. Mina looks down into the lake, and another Mina looks back up at her.

'Konichiwa,' she whispers.

'Ko-ni-chi-wa,' mouths the other Mina.

Now her mum looks back at her from the lake and waves. Mina sees how alike they are, how they are reflected in each other.

'Konichiwa,' they say.

Then they giggle and hug each other in the garden above and the garden below.

Mum goes wandering. Mina sits on a rock by the lake and watches the visitors. A man and boy crouch close by her and peer down into the water as if they're passionately searching for something. Many people do the same, of course, as if the glassy water pulls them to it. When the man and boy stand up, the boy pretends that he's about to dive in. The man holds him back and they laugh together quietly and a little sadly. Then they walk on.

She catches the boy's eye as he passes by.

'Konichiwa,' she whispers, but he's lost in thought.

Mina draws a picture of the temple. She speaks its name, Kinkaku-ji, as she draws, and she writes the name too, so that the image, the word, the sound and its movements are all the same thing.

She writes a tiny note about what happened in the bus:

The packed Kyoto bus. A paper-folding woman. Birds fly from her hands.

She takes a piece of the woman's paper and writes a message on it:

My name is Mina. Whoever finds this will be my friend forever.

She folds the paper edge to edge, point to point. She makes a boat with it. Nowhere near as good as the woman's boat, but something the same. She takes another sheet of paper and folds that, too.

On this she simply writes: *Mina.*

She makes a bird with it, again nowhere near as good but still it's a bird.

She looks at the world, blinks, and looks again. She imagines a whole world made of folded paper: paper temple, paper trees, paper rocks, paper people, all neatly folded and creased in a paper world. She smiles at the lovely illusion.

Then she puts the bird into the boat and stands up.

There are streams flowing through the garden. She kneels beside one of them and carefully places the boat into it and lets it go.

'Sayonara,' she whispers as the boat and the bird are carried away through the rocks and the pine trees. 'Sa-yo-na-ra,' until they've completely gone from sight.

Then her mum's voice:

'Mina! Where are you?'

Mina hurries back to the lake. She waves.

'I'm here!' she calls.

'I'm here,' she calls silently from the world below.

That evening they eat sushi and sashimi and flakes of something that's hardly there at all except for the intensity of the taste it leaves on the tongue. They walk home through the crowds, past the blazing lights of bars and department stores. They're staying in a little timber house in a narrow street near the centre of the town. It's a place with small sparse rooms, low lights, pale gliding shutters, tatami mats on the floors. There's a bathroom with a deep stone bath and with openings in the wall where steam gushes out and a machine for making powdered ice.

In Mina's room a little stone Buddha sits in a shrine with sprigs of cherry blossom and an incense burner. Mina lights the incense and scented smoke drifts through the room. She puts her bird and her boat on the shrine. She lies on a futon on the floor. Her mum's singing in the room next door. The city drones beyond the walls. The moon shines in through the window. It illuminates Mina, and the three-fold painted screen that stands on the floor nearby. Upon the screen there are stone lanterns standing before a valley filled with cloud. There are distant jagged mountains. Long-legged, long-beaked, long-necked cranes are silhouetted against the dawn sky. They appear to be flying through this world towards another or into this world from another.

When she sleeps, she dreams of the bird and the boat that have been carried away. She dreams of being the paper-folding woman. She folds and creases and tugs and teases. She holds her creations in her open hands: look, this is how it's done. Deep into her dreams she makes a dark-haired, dark-eyed boy.

The boy smiles.

Mina smiles back at him.

'Konichiwa,' she says.

Her lips and tongue and breath form the sharp neat shapes and sounds.

'Ko-ni-chi-wa.'

And then she falls into the deep dark silent lake that surrounds us all.

Early next morning, at the edge of Kyoto, the boy is swimming in Biwa Lake. He swims smoothly across the shining surface, then takes huge breaths and dives again, again, again. He loves moving in the depths, with the light above and the darkness below and the silvery flashes of fish around him. He loves to burst out into the air, to curve, to dive down deep again.

This morning there isn't much time. His father's already called him.

'Miyako! Miyako!'

He climbs out onto the bank and crouches at the edge. He bangs two sticks together.

Crack! Crack! Crack!

Black and silver fish rise and gather at the sound.

Crack! Crack! Crack!

'Konichiwa,' he whispers.

He drops crumbs towards their mouths that silently open and close, open and close.

'O O O,' say the fish in silence. 'O O O.'

'Sayonara,' says Miyako.

He's turning away when a little paper boat appears, floating on the surface. He leans down and lifts it out. There's a paper bird inside it.

'Miyako!' calls his father. 'We have to go!'

He stands and sees his father on the narrow beach beside their towels.

'Where are you, Miyako?'

'Look! I'm here, Dad!'

He hurries to him. He dries himself and puts his clothes on. They get into a car, and head into Kyoto.

Miyako inspects the boat and the bird as they travel.

His dad glances at them.

'Origami,' he says. 'And not very good.'

'And very wet,' says Miyako, as the boat collapses between his fingers. He opens it and finds the blotchy faded words inside. He learns English at school, but most of this has seeped into the paper and is pretty meaningless. All he can decipher are the letters that make 'name', 'Mina' and 'ever'.

He finds the message in the bird as well.

'Mina again,' he says.

He refolds the bird and flies it through the tiny spaces around him.

'Careful,' says his dad. 'Don't block my view.'

The streets are packed, the roads are so busy, the traffic's so slow. Dad keeps looking at his watch.

'We'll be late,' he says. 'She'll think we've forgotten about her.'

'Hardly!' says Miyako.

He thinks of the one who wrote the messages. English, maybe. And probably a girl. He flies the bird before his eyes, and it's as if he can still feel the vibrations of its maker within it. He thinks of the girl, and an image of her starts to appear in his mind.

They don't really know it, of course, but as they get close to the centre of Kyoto they slowly pass Mina and her mum, who are standing at a tiny temple that's squashed in between a shoe shop and a bank. They've just rung a bell that hangs from the temple eaves. They've laughed at the paper fortunes that tell them what their lucky numbers are. Mina throws a coin into a small stone pond of golden fish. Miyako watches her. There's something familiar in the way she moves, the way she bows her head. He continues to fly the bird. Mina suddenly turns and sees the boy flying a bird inside a car.

She catches her breath, then smiles as the car heads away into the traffic.

'*Everybody* makes them,' she says.

Soon Miyako's dad drives underground, into a huge downward-spiralling car park. They're down at level 6 before they find a space. Then they hurry to the escalators that zigzag through a huge department store towards the sky.

Sakura's at a table in the open roof café. She has a pot of coffee with two cups, and a glass of lemonade. She stands when she sees them, bows and smiles. Miyako's dad is all apologies, but she takes his hand and says it's nothing, it's okay.

'Good morning, Miyako,' she says. 'You have been in the water today?'

'Yes,' he says.

She indicates the lemonade.

'For you,' she says.

He thanks her. They're still awkward with each other. Miyako plays with the bird as she and his dad talk and laugh about some mysterious theatre they saw together.

Miyako unfolds the bird and writes his name beside the name of Mina. He makes the bird again, then slips away from the table and goes to the parapet. He looks back. Sakura's okay, he supposes. His dad's laughing again. Change is coming, he knows that.

Miyako looks down over beautiful Kyoto: the crowded streets, the skyscrapers, the flashing lights, the gardens. He sees Kinkaku-ji itself. He's even sure he can see its reflection in the water. He holds the bird above the parapet and flicks his wrist and lets it fly.

Mina and her mum walk happily arm-in-arm. Mina's imagining, as she often does, that her dad is walking beside her, too. Mum's bought a print of Mount Fuji rising from the mist. Mina's bought some manga, two versions of the same story contained within one book. The English version starts from the left, the Japanese from the right. The versions end and come together at the centre.

Mina and her mum love the crowds, the shops, the buses, the food, the temples. They love the silence and stillness at the heart of it all. It's the last day. Tomorrow it's a bullet train to Hiroshima. But they feel that even when they've left this place they'll still be here.

Mina looks up as they walk and here's the bird, swaying, falling, spinning, flying, a single tiny bird in all that space, a single tiny bird in space that goes on forever, as far as distant England, as far as the furthest star.

Mina raises her hands and the points of the bird touch the points of her fingers. She neatly folds her hands around it, then opens them, and shows it resting there.

'It can't be,' says her mum.

But it is. Mina opens the bird, and there's her name, with the new unreadable beautiful word by its side.

They look up into the emptiness. There's nothing they can say.

They walk on through indecipherable Kyoto.

Miyako and his dad and Sakura come down on the zigzag escalators. Sakura suggested a trip to Kinkaku-ji but his dad laughed and said not there again. So they're heading for McDonald's and the cinema. Miyako knows they're doing it for him. That's okay. He's starting to feel at ease with her. He's even starting to like her, and to feel happy for his dad.

They walk through the sea of people. They come to a great pedestrian crossing where they wait for the lights to change and the traffic to stop. Mina and her mum are waiting at the far side.

The moment comes and the tides of people flow towards each other in the crowded city beneath the empty sky.

Mina and Miyako see each other.

They stop, and bring the adults who are with them to a stop as well.

'Konichiwa!' says Miyako.

'Ko-ni-chi-wa!' says Mina.

SHENANDOAH

by FRANK COTTRELL BOYCE

MUM AND ME are writing this whole thing down because we don't want anyone to get into trouble. By the time anyone reads this, we will have vanished. But don't worry about it. We vanished ourselves.

It's not like anyone ever noticed we were there to start with. For instance, because I like to get the same bus as Mum – and because her shift starts at 7.30 – I always get to school before anyone else. Before the Breakfast Club opens. Before Mrs Teague even gets there, which is at 7.45. She never notices me sitting on the wall near Reception because she's always on her phone. I wasn't the first to get there last Monday though. Last Monday, there was already a big old minibus with foreign plates and millions of bumps in the bodywork, like it had been caught in an asteroid storm. It was parked right across two parking spaces. And one of them was Mrs Teague's. When she saw this, she pocketed her phone for once and stared really hard at the driver. But the driver was asleep and staring didn't wake her up.

Then Mrs Teague noticed me for the first time ever.

'What's this?' she said.

I had actually been thinking what it might be so I said, 'French Exchange maybe?' French Exchange is when some students from a school in France come to stay and then some of us go back with them to France.

'There's nothing in the diary. Where are you from?'

'From here.'

'No, no, no. What. Country. Are. You. From? What school? There's nothing in the diary.'

'From this school. I'm from this school.'

'I don't think you understand. And sadly I don't speak French. Well, well, *quelle domage*. Mrs Grady speaks French. Because she's the French teacher...'

'I know.' Mrs Grady is my French teacher.

'She'll be here shortly. She'll sort out the details. You. Are. Very. Welcome to our school.'

'Thanks.'

The fact that Mrs Teague thought I was with the French kids somehow made me feel that I should wait with the minibus instead of going to Breakfast Club. After a while the French kids got out of the minibus, swung their arms, stretched their legs, ran on the spot and smiled at me. They didn't look one little bit French. Maybe it had been a long journey but their hair was really messy, and they were wearing bright blue tracksuity things and carrying massive backpacks. Then Mrs Grady showed up, looking like she was going to disintegrate from stress. She was soooo sorry, soooo sorry, she said, because there had been some sort of mix-up. The French girls weren't expected until June.

All the French girls stared at her and then stared at me, like I was going to translate for them. Then one of them said 'June' and they all said 'June' and then they said it again a few times and Mrs Grady said, '*Oui, oui, mais pas de problème. Vous êtes toujours bienvenus a notre école.*'

The French kids stared at her again and their stares were absolutely blank. 'Oh dear,' said Mrs Grady, 'Maybe it's my accent.' Then she looked at me and said, 'Please. Come. With. Me. To. My. Class.'

'I always come to your class. I'm in your class. I'm Shania.'

'Yes, yes. My class. Come. This way. *Suivez-vous.*'

The French kids seemed to like the French class. Every time Mrs Grady asked us to repeat something in French, they repeated it. And kept repeating it. All morning. No matter what the lesson was. And mostly in unison. In Geography, when Mr Norman turned round to write the word 'solifluction' on the white board, they all went, '*Bonjooooouuur*'. He dropped his sharpie in surprise then he said '*Bonjour*' back. And they said '*Bonjooooouuur*' back to him and he said '*Bonjour*' back and it did look like that might go on all morning. But then the bell went for break and everyone piled out. Except the French kids who stood there smiling at me. Apparently I was in charge of them now.

I was already beginning to suspect that they weren't French.

Maybe if I took them to the library I could show them an atlas or something and they could show me where they were from.

I said, 'Let's go to the library.'

'*Bonjooouuur*,' they said.

I showed them France in the atlas but it didn't seem to interest them. Neither did Germany. Neither did Europe. Neither did the northern hemisphere. The only thing they liked was the index. They ran their fingers down the tiny printed place names saying, 'Addis Ababa' and 'Minsk' and 'Shenandoah.'

Then they got distracted because Olivia was playing *Labyrinth* on one of the computers. They stood there watching for a while as the little Greek soldier went running around, bumping into walls, falling over and being chased by the Minotaur. Finally, the Minotaur got him and they all burst into tears. Not sparkly little sniffy tears, by the way. Big bawling howling tears mixed with mucus. They hugged each other, shuddering with sorrow. I tried to explain that it was alright – Olivia still had nine lives left.

'Look,' I said, 'The soldier's back. He's back at the beginning.'

Somehow that just made them louder and more grief stricken. The librarian came and tried to tell them off but they couldn't hear her over the sobs and woe, so she sent for Mrs Grady. Mrs Grady said it was nothing to do with her because they weren't French. At which point one of them looked at the screen and cried, '*Au revoir!*' and they all shouted '*Au revoir!*'

'They're speaking French,' said the librarian.

'But if I speak French to them they don't understand.'

'It's probably your accent.'

Mrs Grady looked at me and said, '*Quelle est le problème?*'

I said, 'I'm not French, Miss.'

'There,' she said, 'What did I tell you. They're not French. They're not French so they're not my responsibility. Now if you'll excuse me, I've got netball.'

In the end, Mrs Teague came and said maybe it was best if they had an early lunch.

Normal lunch is this: you queue up, you look in the big metal trays to see what there is, then you give the dinner lady your plate and she serves you. That's not how the 'French' did it. They queued up and then started tasting things from the trays. When the dinner lady tried to stop them they all said, 'Shenandoah' or 'Belarus'. Then they took a big tray of chips over to a table, and ate them in big handfuls. After that they opened their enormous backpacks, took out sleeping bags, lay down in a corner of the hall and went to sleep. They snored loudly.

'What's going on here!?' said the chief dinner lady.

'They're from Europe,' said Mrs Teague. 'They have to have a siesta. It's part of the culture. Quiet, everybody. The French are sleeping.' A little bit later I found out that they'd left a wad of money on the table 'as a tip'. Two hundred quid apparently.

Mrs Teague spotted me and said, 'Normally during these exchange visits, the visiting school goes out for the afternoon and takes a look around the city.'

'You want me to go out with them for the afternoon?'

'Very much so.'

So. I knew that if I walked out to their minibus when they woke up, they'd follow me. Which they did. I thought it might be nice to pick Mum up from work (she finishes about two) and give her a lift home or maybe even go for a day out. I'd like to say I was a bit surprised that one of the girls got into the driving seat and started the engine, but I was beyond surprise by then. I pointed the way to the Children's Hospital, and we got there just as Mum was arriving at her bus stop.

'Very nice to meet you,' she said as she climbed on board. 'Where are you all from?'

Replies ranged from Minsk and Addis Ababa to Shenandoah.

'Oh, Shenandoah I long to see you,' sang Mum. 'I love that song. It's so sad. Although I can't really tell what it's all about. I mean is Shenandoah a river or a girl. And is he going home or leaving home?' She sang a little bit more: 'Far away, you rolling river! Oh Shenandoah, my heart is near you...' She had to stop though because the girls all burst into tears again.

'They're very emotional, aren't they?' whispered Mum. 'Where are they from?'

I said, 'They're French.'

'They don't look French. Their hair's too messy.'

'I can't figure out where they're from.'

'I'm sure I can figure it out,' said Mum. 'I've met people from every place under the sun working in the Children's Hospital.' She listened while they talked and wrote down the odd word.

'I'm supposed to take them somewhere interesting, show them our culture but I can't think of anywhere.'

'Safari Park, obviously,' said Mum. Which was exactly the right answer because we always wanted to go there, but you need a car to go there and we don't have one. Also because it's quite expensive and they've got loads of money. But most of all because it's full of large grazing animals that poo a lot and it turned out that the French kids thought that poo was the funniest thing on earth. Every time a buffalo or a gazelle lifted up its tail, they pointed and started laughing and shouting, 'Minsk! Minsk! Ha ha ha ha ha.'

I loved the Safari Park. The monkeys climbed all over the car and wrenched the windscreen wipers off, which was hilarious. The only bit that troubled me was the lions. The lions crowded round the car, with their massive heads and their heavy paws and their eyes which didn't show any expression, as though they were invisible. I was so hypnotised by them that at first I didn't notice the 'French' were climbing out of the van and going for the lions. I saw them fanning out and holding their arms wide, yipping and yowling. I couldn't look after that. I didn't want to see them being ripped limb from limb. I covered my face with my hands. I heard lions roaring. Then I heard French girls laughing. I suppose that meant that one of the lions had done a poo. Then we drove on. There didn't seem to be any dismembered limbs or severed heads in the car so I suppose that somehow they got away with it.

Normally during French Exchange, each French student stays with an English family. No one had sorted this out. Maybe they would all have to stay with us. But no. They stopped outside our house and when we looked round, they'd gone.

'They must have made other arrangements for overnight accommodation. It's a shame. They would have been very welcome,' said Mum. 'They seemed very cheery. I've written down loads of the words they said. Tomorrow I'll ask around the hospital and see if anyone recognises any of them. I'm betting on Finland. Or Hungary. Finnish is not related to other European languages.'

I found out what their 'other arrangements' were the next morning.

×

When I got up, Mum was just sitting at the table with her phone in one hand and the list of words she'd made in the other.

'Let's go,' I said.

'I'm not going anywhere,' said Mum, still staring straight in front of her.

'Why?'

She pushed the phone across the table towards me. She'd been sacked. By text.

'Twenty-three years, I've worked there,' she said. 'They didn't even spell my name right.'

I didn't want to leave her. But it would have been a bit weird, I suppose, taking your Mum to school. 'Maybe the Finnish girls will want to go out again,' I said. 'We'll come round at lunchtime. You think of somewhere nice.'

×

If you were worried about how the Finnish or French or Whatever kept warm and dry overnight, don't be. They built themselves a massive shelter out of branches with leaves for the roof. It looked amazing. Like a South Pacific longhouse. Everyone loved it at first. Then someone noticed that all the trees were missing from the school playing fields.

'Who would steal ten birch trees and a clump of sycamores?' said Olivia. Then she looked at the shelter and said, 'Oh,' and 'I see.' The visitors had chopped down all the trees from around the school and built a bonfire out of the ones they hadn't used for their longhouse.

'Bonjour!' they said when they saw me.

Mrs Teague was annoyed. 'This is a conservation area,' she said. 'You need permission from the council to cut-down trees…'

'Permission, yes,' smiled the biggest girl. 'We would like permission to present an assembly this morning to tell you all about who we are and what we have learned.'

'Oh,' said Mrs Teague. 'You speak English. I didn't realise.'

'You didn't ask,' said Etta.

I followed closely behind her. I said, 'Where did you learn to speak English?'

'Just picked up a bit here and there. It's all about listening,' said Etta. 'Stand at the back of the hall, near the exits, during the assembly.'

'Why?'

'Honestly, don't talk. Just listen.'

Assembly was all about Listening. Etta said she had seen many people talking, talking, talking since she came to school. 'People,'

she said, 'even talk to their dogs!'

The other Finnish or French or Whatever girls laughed loud and long.

'That won't work!' said Etta. 'We listen. This is why we learn so much. So much about you all. Thank you. You should listen too. Yesterday for instance we saw a creature in the safari park and we listened to him. Here he is now for you to listen to...'

And two of the French or Finnish or Whatever girls came yipping and yowling and howling onto the stage, driving the lion before them. The lion may have roared. I'm not sure. Like most people, I didn't stay around to listen. I practically teleported myself back to that minibus.

'Where to today?' said Etta.

'Can we pick up Mum?'

We picked up Mum. She was still sitting where I left her, still with the phone in her hand.

'Can we go back to the Safari Park?' she said. 'This time maybe I could play with the lions.'

'No. I don't think we should do that. I think we should go somewhere quiet and calm. Like the Art Gallery.'

The Art Gallery was quiet and calm until the French or Finnish or Whatever girls got there. The moment they saw the painting *The Death of Nelson*, they were off weeping and wailing and sobbing again. They cried themselves into a mush. *The Execution of Lady Jane Grey* was worse. They screamed and pointed at the axe about to fall on Lady Jane's neck so loud that you thought the painted axe man would stop and history would change. Mum knew what to do obviously. She took them into the abstract gallery and they sat smiling calmly at a big canvas covered in yellow splodges. 'Twenty million quid that cost,' said Mum.

'Worth every penny,' said Etta.

The next morning they wanted to give another assembly. Mrs Teague didn't really want to let them back onto the school premises. It had taken two helicopters and a team of police marksmen to deal with the lion and no matter what Mrs Teague said, the police seemed to think it was all her fault.

'I think it's probably time you went home,' she said.

'We don't have a lion with us today,' said Etta.

Mrs Teague looked at Etta's backpack as if there might be a lion in there somewhere.

'We have a present for you.'

Mrs Teague obviously remembered the massive tip. She said okay.

Assembly was about being calm and only thinking about bad things. 'Just don't think about bad things!' yelled Etta. 'Stop it! It makes you bad. You have bad things on your posters – vampires and stuff – and gloomy things on your records. Stop! Listen to good things. For instance...'

And they all started singing 'Shenandoah'. 'Oh Shenandoah I long to hear you... far away you rolling river...'

They sang so beautifully and it sounded so sad. Mum was right you couldn't tell whether Shenandoah was a girl or a river. But you could tell what it meant. It meant that home was far away and that the singer wished he was there. When the girls sang it, with tears in their eyes, it meant, *away, we're bound away back to the place we love.* I texted Mum and told her to get over to the school quickly.

'… Oh Shenandoah I long to hear you. Away, I'm bound away 'cross the wide Missouri…' Everyone's spine was tingling when they finished.

'Also,' said Etta, 'look at happy things.' And she presented Mrs Teague with the yellow splodges worth £20 million. And stood smiling at the painting for the longest time while the French or Finnish or Whatever girls went outside.

'Thanks for all your trouble,' said Etta and handed Mum a big wad of cash.

'You speak English!' said Mum.

'Un peu,' said Etta.

'Where are you from?' asked Mum. Why hadn't I thought of that!?

'A little place. You wouldn't know it.'

'The thing is,' said Mum, 'if this is a student exchange, you should take someone with you.'

'Hop onboard,' said Etta. We hopped onboard.

'This may take a while,' smiled Etta. So we wrote this note while the engine warmed up. It did take a while. We were surprised to see the whole minibus tipping backwards onto its rear wheels. Also surprising was the fact that everyone was given an oxygen mask – for a ride in a minibus!? There's a big crowd on the playground watching us. We're going to pass one of them this note and then we're vanishing ourselves. We don't know where we're going but by the time you read this… we will be dust.

NOTE – taken from the Reuters press agency: *Mrs S Teague – the headmistress at the centre of the 'lion on the hockey pitch' incident – was today arrested for the theft of a masterpiece of modern art worth £20m. Her defence 'It wasn't me it was some French kids who jumped into a minivan which then just vanished into thin air' was at first dismissed by police attending the crime. But mobile phone footage has come to light of what appears to be a minibus taking off from the playground, flying into the air and ascending into the stratosphere 'like some alien craft.'*

WELCOME TO FLAXLAND!

by ANDY STANTON

FLAXLAND! THE VERY name conjures up images of romantic midnight trysts, tiny state-subsidised oranges, and somebody saying 'Flaxland'. If it's colourful hustle and bustle you're after then look no further than the many historic market towns which litter the interior like so many undiscovered trinkets. If magnificent architecture, ancient tombs and follies are more your style then an embarrassment of riches awaits. Or perhaps you'd just like to relax in a big pool, safe in the knowledge that a hamburger is making its way to you on a trolley. Whatever it is that you seek, nowhere does the paradox of culture, art, the grindstone of tradition meeting the dynamic impetus for communication, is better and more clearly expressed than in this 'country of changes'.

HISTORY

Originally a trading post for monks selling relics (e.g. bone of saint, piece of one true cross, sandal) and fruit (e.g. melon), Flaxland's centralised position and extensive network of bushes soon made it clear that it would be a nice place to live, not only for monks but for normal people too. In 1302 the first settlers arrived and built a house of wood. This house still survives today, in the sense that its atoms exist somewhere in the universe. Sadly the house itself is long gone. Indeed, it is probable that there was not even a house to begin with.

The first settlers were known as 'El Ninos Tarangeos', or 'the Fat Men from the South'. Realising that the key to their success lay in the rich fertile soil of the region, they carted it away bit by bit to be sold on at a quick profit to neighbouring states. As a result of this, the land rapidly became arid and has remained largely unsuitable for farming ever since. In all respects, life in the fourteenth century was harsh and unforgiving: of the two hundred and forty men, women and children who originally came to the settlement, not a single one is alive today.

In 1360, King Carlos XIICMXCLXII of Catalonia visited the fledgling country and wrote of it:

It is a mean sort of a place, dispiriting and distasteful to the senses. If I had to rate it on a scale of one to ten, where one is not very fetid and ten is extremely fetid, I should probably give it an eight.

However, he later revised his poor opinion, giving it a nine.

Until the end of the sixteenth century Flaxland was a feudal state, ruled over by an elite group of barons and princes who enjoyed a life of carefree idleness while their serfs laboured thanklessly on the land. But the Renaissance was to change all that. Now the barons and princes enjoyed a life working on paintings and classical statues while their serfs laboured thanklessly on the land.

For Flaxland, the Renaissance was truly an age of wonders, of things that had not been heretofore witnessed being envisaged in the mind's eye and then painted with bristles on canvas stretched upon the easel of progress, the word made flesh in a collective easing of the imaginative bowel that rained down upon the internal landscape of the nation like a cleansing brown rain.

One of the most famous paintings from the period is Giuverchi's *El Ninos Tarangeos* ('Adonis in the Forest'), which now hangs in the Flaxland National Gallery. It is superb, most of the trees are more or less the right sort of shape. Other well-known works of the Flaxonian Renaissance include a sculpture of Adam and Eve, a painting of the sculpture and a sculpture of the painting of the sculpture which one modern commentator has called 'mindless'.

The fashion for art and gentle reflection was not to last. In 1730 the nation's paintbrushes were swapped for swords: the Flaxland Civil War had begun, exactly as predicted by the great seer Streptococcus two days earlier. It was to rage for nearly twenty years, an almost unimaginable length of time. To put it into context, that is almost 631,138,519 seconds; or as long as sixteen dozen double-decker buses. The death toll was tremendous. It was so awful that some people actually died twice.

Early on in the conflict, the King was deposed by an angry mob and fled to northern France. However, he was not yet beaten. Becoming a carpenter, he fashioned tables with deliberately uneven legs, and began exporting them back to his home country in a slow but persistent campaign against his detractors. This ruse eventually bore fruit: finding that their plans and charts would not stay put on the lop-sided table tops, the revolutionaries were forced to concede defeat. They had been thwarted, and in 1719 the King rode back home to reclaim his crown, bringing the whole unfortunate episode to an end. Gradually the country returned to everyday life – but its people had suffered much and a certain innocence had been lost forever. A war memorial in the shape of a dancing clown was erected in Parliament Square, symbolising the bitterness of conflict. It still stands there today, a poignant reminder of a tragic time.

After that, nothing much happened for a couple of hundred years.

FLAXLAND LORE AND LEGEND

It is often said of Flaxland that it is a magical place and nowhere is this truer than in the many caves and grottos that honeycomb the north-east coast. Mile for mile these geological marvels contain more apparitions than anywhere else on earth. Of course, not all of the phantoms are benevolent; some are downright menacing. But overall they are a friendly lot and should a traveller find himself stranded she will often be taken in for the night and treated to spectacular displays of phosphorescent emanations and necromancy.

The most famous of all the cave's supernatural residents is El Ninos Tarangeos (literally, 'the Inside-Out Soldier'), whose ghastly appearance is belied by his gentle nature and knowledge of the local flora. But don't be fooled by his gentle nature and knowledge of the local flora – one false move and you'll be dead, yet another victim of his snapping teeth. Also, some of the caves are poisonous. No, all of them.

For centuries, Flaxland was terrorised by witches who used the country as a convenient stopping-off point on their long annual migrations. Souring milk, unsouring sour cream and wreaking absolute havoc on the cheeses of the region, it seemed impossible to stop these pests. However, in 1873 a solution was found in the form of a small placard placed in a field:

Please do not come here if you are a witch.

Ever since then Flaxland has been witch-free, a fact of which it is justifiably proud. As for other marvellous creatures, the evidence is scant at best. Rumours persist of microscopic giants in the western marches but at the time of writing these remain unconfirmed. Many of the smaller villages have reported 'anti-vampires', strange creatures said to pump domestic animals and livestock full of blood and vitamin supplements; but the people here are very superstitious and these entities may in fact be nothing more than common vets.

ENTERTAINMENT & NIGHTLIFE

None.

CUISINE

The national dish is 'El Ninos Tarangeos', or 'the Plate of Beasts'. Typically this is served in a large ceramic tureen and will contain a smorgasbord of good local meats: wild rabbit, goat, hell-fly, chicken, beef and pork are most usual. The dish varies according to region and setting. In an expensive restaurant you might find it supplemented with fish roe, venison and smoked ham; in a small mountain cantina it will often be garnished with any old crap they can get hold of. As the dish is enjoyed by all levels of society it is sometimes referred to as 'El Ninos Tarangeos' ('The Ladder That Connects Us All').

Seafood is fresh and plentiful. Take care with oysters as some will literally burst into flame when tackled. The native species of crab is not recommended as it is capable of reincarnating in your stomach and exacting a stormy vengeance. Dory, tuna and marlin are all good. If you know the right people you can get whale meat.

Nuts, seeds and berries are known but frowned upon. Tea is gritty and sweet, and will contain either a fragment of Rubik's Cube or a swathe of Velcro, depending on who is in power. Fleshy and delectable, the local strain of melon dates back to the days of the monks and is an absolute must.

One peculiarity of Flaxland dining is that restaurateurs will often require you to stand at the base of a high wall while they lower your food into your mouth on lengths of string. Additionally, it is considered *de rigueur* for children to pay the bill.

The Flaxonian attitude to vegetarians is complex. In some parts of the country vegetarianism is viewed as a mild perversion, akin to cross-dressing or licking the inside of a freezer. Having said this, chefs are by and large tolerant and will usually endeavour to rustle something up in a pinch. Vegans are not allowed into the country under any circumstances.

One word of warning: on no account try the local strain of melon.

GETTING AROUND, CURRENCY, COMMUNICATIONS

In Flaxland there is a saying: 'You either go by car, train, bus, boat, plane, bicycle, motorbike, jet ski, hovercraft, walk or get around some other way.' Public transport is cheap but can be notoriously unreliable. Flaxonian bus drivers are absolutely fascinated by new experiences and exist in a state of wide-eyed wonder at the world, frequently driving their vehicles off cliff-tops for the thrill of it or stopping en route to perform impromptu drum solos lasting deep into the early hours. Trains are a safer bet but can be somewhat gassy. Hitchhiking is not a good idea as, under state law, anyone getting into a private vehicle becomes the lifelong property of the vehicle's owner.

Since 2006, the national currency is the Euro. As a rule of thumb one Flaxonian Euro is worth about 0.8 Euros. Be prepared to barter for goods and services, sometimes for days. Running out of shops clutching items you haven't paid for is a definite no-no.

Telephone calls in Flaxland are charged according to the distance between the two parties, so if you are making a long-distance call it will pay to walk a few miles up the road first. Be aware that the government intercepts all emails and that they will often change some of your words and phrases for a joke; many is the visitor to Flaxland who has returned to their homeland to be asked what they meant by 'that remark about the elephant and the priest'. In the event of an emergency the nearest British Consulate is located in Lisbon.

So there you have it! We wish you all the very best during your stay and hope you enjoy your time here in this fascinating and enchanting place. To paraphrase the country's greatest living writer, Bastiferus (1830-1892):

All of life is… here… in the… place where… it… floater… cross of Jesus… is… not decided… rake.

A world of wonders awaits. Welcome to 'Europe's hidden jewel'. Welcome to Flaxland!

SOME USEFUL PHRASES

Hello – *Nistra*
Goodbye – *Nistraa*
Please – *Nistraaa*
Thank you – *Nistraaaa*
Cement mixer – *El Ninos Tarangeos*

THE ELSEWHERE GENIE

JOHN FARDELL

There was once an island...

...which had only two inhabitants:

an ogre, and his slave.
Slave! Where's my dinner?
Here, master.

Now scrub the floors, fix the roof, clean the toilet, and then do the washing up.
Yes, master.

One day...
Slave! Have you polished all the silverware yet?
Nearly, master.

I hate it here. I wish I could live elsewhere.
RUB RUB

BLAM!

I am the Elsewhere Genie. I can transport you to anywhere you wish to go.

However, I can only grant one wish per person, so choose carefully.

Gosh! Where to choose? Trouble is, I don't know anywhere else.

How about that island on the horizon? At least I'd be free from the ogre.

Your wish is my command.

SHAZAM!

PING!
Wow! It worked!
Uh? Where have you come from?

I came from that island over there, by magic. There's a genie in this jug.

Well, it's nice to have your company after being stranded here by myself for so long. But you've chosen a terrible island to come to. It's cold, damp, rocky, and infested by *scary giant crabs*.

Can your genie transport us somewhere else?

He can only grant one wish per person. But here — you have a go.

OK, but I'm not leaving you behind.

RUB RUB

You called?

Genie, I wish for you to transport both of us to that nice-looking green, bushy island over there.

Granted.

SHAZAM!

PING!

Uh? How did you get here?

We came by magic.

Can we live here?

You wouldn't want to live here...

The whole island is ruled by carnivorous dinosaurs! I'm the only monkey left!

Uh-oh! He's seen us! Quick, monkey — summon the genie!

BROOK CROOKS

by KEITH GRAY

THEY'D BUILT THIS massive gate. And the first thing I thought was, Who'd want to break into Brook High? Then I thought about Panny and Phil wanting to break *out*, and that made me laugh. Full-on Alcatraz-style escape stuff. Dodging searchlights, teachers with rifles at the staffroom windows. I reckoned Panny would make it to freedom but Phil was a dead man, a bullet in the back of the head – he'd never been able to run three metres without needing to stop for a ciggie and a burger.

The gate surprised me. I'd been thirteen when Dad just upped and decided to drag us right across the other side of the country and into the middle of nowhere. And maybe not everything would be 100% exactly the same after two years, but I'd had it in my head I was going to walk right into the school, just wander into whatever lesson Panny and Phil were having, and sit down at a desk next to them like I'd never even been gone. Surprise! They'd think it was the funniest thing ever. The teachers would go ballistic. I grinned massively as I thought about the looks on Panny's and Phil's faces – just full-on priceless. It'd be Kenzie, Panny and Phil, the *Brook Crooks*, back together again.

The gate was locked. I stuck my head through the bars and at least the school on the other side was the same as I remembered. Maybe most people would call it ugly but after being stuck in the middle of nowhere for so long I reckoned Brook's grey boxes looked fantastic – because I knew it all so well.

Raymond Aveis Brook's back entrance and it had always been just a gap in a shabby hedge – shabby because me, Panny and Phil shoved kids like Toby Mitten through it at least twice a day. The people who lived along here had always kept complaining about noise and bikes on the pavement and litter and stuff. I reckoned it was them who'd got the gate put up. It probably forced everybody to use the main entrance on Straub Street, even though it was the further way around for anyone who lived this side of the estate.

It was starting to rain, just spitting, but I never used to walk the long way before and didn't want to do it now. I didn't see why I had to change. So for old times' sake I climbed the gate.

I was halfway up when someone hammered on a window. I was quick to jump down.

This old man in the front window of the nearest house shouted at me like I was a dog.

'Down! Down!'

You know that patch in the middle of a leather chair, collapsed and saggy and creased from too many fat backsides? That's what his face looked like. He waved a phone at me, threatening to call the police or school or whoever.

'Down! Down!'

I pointed at my feet. 'I'm down, aren't I?' I held out my hands like, What's your problem?

I took my own sweet time to zip my coat all the way up under my chin, push my hands into my pockets, and kick at some loose tarmac stones. Then when I decided I could be bothered, I slouched away up the middle of the road, letting him watch me go.

But as soon as I turned the corner I ran. I wanted to get to the main entrance before school finished. I knew Panny and Phil were always quick off the mark getting out.

I've been going on at Mum to let me come back for ages. The thing is, my new school, I reckon it's a school for weirdoes and arseholes. It's this tiny, little school in this tiny, little middle-of-nowhere village, middle-of-nowhere county. Postcode: N0 WH3R3. But it's definitely the school to go to if you want to learn how to be a bigger arsehole.

And the biggest of all is Mickey Thomas – full-on capital A, capital H. It's like he's the one who gets to decide who's 'in' and who's *cool* and who has their bag nicked and filled with cow crap from his dad's farmyard twice a week. But his idea of cool is so weird – he knows the names of different tractors. After two years he still calls me 'New Kid' and 'City Dick' and copies my accent. Or what he thinks is my accent.

He's big – massive enough he can carry a cow in each hand. He reckons he bites the heads off chickens. He makes up his own rules too, like: Anyone wearing blue trainers on a Tuesday has to pay him £5. But only after he's already seen me in my favourite Adidas. So either I pay him or I end up walking around in just my socks all day. The other kids go along with him, thinking he's funny. I just don't get it. It's like the school is this whole other place and all upside down to how it should be.

I've tried to get in with Mickey. I've tried to like tractors. I've told him about some of the things me, Panny and Phil have done. Like when we super-glued a maths book to Toby Mitten's face. The teachers said he always had his head stuck in a book – we just pinned him down and made it come true.

Me, Panny and Phil call ourselves the *Brook Crooks* but we only ever mucked about for a laugh. Mickey Thomas only ever seems happy when he's making my life a full-on nightmare, in his nightmare school, in his upside-down weird elsewhere world.

Dad doesn't care that he's thrown me into this messed-up place where I don't know anything, that's obvious. Both him and Mum talk to me like I'm still ten. They haven't totally banned me from keeping in touch with Panny and Phil but I only use the school's email, just in case. Mum only got freaked out about stuff at Brook because she went snooping in my inbox and no way am I going to trust her now. Who knows what middle-of-nowhere place Dad's going to want to move to next time.

But I don't tell Panny and Phil everything. What I say is some of the stuff that Mickey Thomas does to me, just make out it's me and Mickey doing it to someone else.

I made it to Brook's main entrance the second the bell went, sweaty but glad I'd run.

Two seconds later people started pouring out onto Straub Street. The rain wasn't that bad but most people had hoods or caps or brollies. Some of the teachers were as desperate to get away as the kids, honking their car horns to chase dawdlers out of the middle of the road. I reckoned keeping that new gate at Raymond Ave locked just clogged up these gates here.

I worried I might not see Panny and Phil in amongst it all. What if I missed them? I'd come all this way. They might not even be at school today. Maybe they were having an *Xbox* Day, crashed out on Phil's floor.

Thinking that made me massively jealous. The best days had been when Phil said something like, 'Let's vote about tomorrow. Personal Development Studies with Mrs McHenry, or an *Xbox* Day?'

Maybe I missed *Xbox* days most of all. The three of us just shooting stuff up, larking about, hanging around – no teachers, parents, arseholes. Full-on best mates.

I reckoned I should ask someone if they knew Panny or Phil and if they'd seen them around today. Or if I could borrow someone's mobile so I could text them. I knew Phil's number off-by-heart. But it felt weird that there were so many people I didn't recognise – all younger kids who'd started Brook after I'd left.

But then I spotted an umbrella held higher than anybody else's. I only knew one person that tall.

'Panny!'

At least I thought it was Panny.

'Panny!'

It was him, definitely. But he'd done something stupid to his hair – like he was trying to look like a pop star. I shoved against the flow of kids.

'Hey! Panny!'

I got a kick out of how surprised he looked. 'Kenzie? What're you doing here?'

'I'm back for the weekend, aren't I? Staying at my uncle's.' I grinned up at him. 'Trust me, where I live, and my school – it's driving me full-on insane. I needed to get back to Brook just to save my life.' I stood there like a big grinning puppy-dog idiot and had to have a word with myself to calm down. 'Where's fat-boy Phil anyway? Nicking someone's burgers and pies?'

Panny glanced back over his shoulder. 'Dunno. He'll probably be out soon, I think he was in today.' He saw I looked confused and shrugged under his brolly. 'We don't really hang around much anymore.'

I knew he was joking, so laughed.

He shrugged again. 'I've got to go. I'm meeting my girlfriend.'

I laughed harder. Hoping he was still joking. 'Come on, the three of us back together. It's like a reunion tour, yeah? We can get Toby Mittens, make him cry for old times' sake.'

Panny looked at me like I was the one not making sense. 'I'm meeting Harriet.'

'Harriet?' I only knew one Harriet. 'You're seeing Harriet Festival? With the massive chestivals?'

'Don't say that.'

'We always call her Harriet Chestivals.'

'When we were twelve, maybe.'

'Is she why you've got your hair all – ?' I reached out as if to ruffle it. I was only messing, and was far too short to even reach that high. But he slapped my hand away – hard.

He glared at me. Then patted and finger-combed his flicky fringe to make sure I hadn't ruined any of his style.

We stood there in the rain. He didn't look right with an umbrella but I didn't want to say so. Other kids flowed past us.

I said, 'I'm not back long. Maybe –'

'I promised Harriet.'

'Just un-promise her.'

He shook his head. 'Call me tomorrow if you want.'

'I've not got my phone on me.' It was in Mickey Thomas's back pocket. Or under his tractor's back wheel. Or up a cow's backside. Somewhere I'd never see it again anyway.

Panny shrugged.

We stood there in the rain.

'I just thought it'd be a laugh,' I said, still wanting to win him over. 'Me, you and Phil – *Brook Crooks* reunited.'

At last he smiled. 'Brook Crooks. Right. I forgot you used to call us that.'

How could he forget? It was all I ever thought about out there in the middle of nowhere. 'So, come on,' I pushed. 'Tonight, we could –'

'I promised Harriet. Call me tomorrow, yeah?'

I didn't remind him about my phone because he was already lost in the flow of kids through the gates, holding his brolly close to his head to protect his stupid hair. I couldn't believe I was really seeing the real Panny run off like that. The real Panny didn't give a shit about girls – or hair.

Not that I was going to give up. If anybody could make the real Panny appear – like magic, like a mad rabbit out of a fancy hat – Phil could. I just had to find him.

But he found me.

A hand clamped down on my shoulder making me jump. A voice shrieked into my ear, '*Stranger danger! Stranger danger!*'

My grin was so full-on massive it could have split my head in two.

'Hey, Kenzie.' He was grinning too. 'What're you doing back?'

But my grin fell off – just splashed to the ground. Because it was a total shock. Fat Phil was thin.

'Wow,' I said, choosing my words carefully. 'Where's the rest of you?' He laughed. I didn't. He looked like a right gym-jockey. The one chin he had left was like a chunk of brick. I said, 'Seriously, you've changed. Why aren't you fat?'

He rolled his eyes. 'Why aren't you pretty?'

I still didn't laugh. He'd been funny when he was fat. Now he just seemed thin and sarcastic.

We were jostled by kids pushing past. I shoved back, getting annoyed.

Phil said, 'Listen, thanks for all your emails. Sorry I haven't replied much. Sounds like you're having a full-on time with your mate, though, yeah? Mickey? I can't believe how lucky you are escaping this place.'

I didn't know what he meant, but didn't want him knowing the truth either. 'I saw Panny. Did you know he's got an umbrella?'

Phil rolled his eyes again. 'Yeah. Who'd have guessed he even knew how to work one, right?'

'He said you don't hang around much anymore.'

'Things've changed, I suppose.'

'I haven't.'

'I can tell.'

I didn't like the way he said it, and wasn't sure if he was being thinly sarcastic, so ignored it. 'I reckon we should get together though, yeah? While I'm back. You could get Panny to meet us, couldn't you? Get together for an *Xbox* day or something?'

'Don't see why not. Could be a laugh.'

'Course it'll be a laugh.' And I laughed loudly to prove it. 'A massive laugh. Full-on.' I decided he might be weird-looking thin-Phil on the outside, but he was still *Phil* Phil inside. '*Brook Crooks* back together again.'

He laughed so hard he actually rocked back on his heels. 'How d'you remember all this stuff?'

I could have asked, How d'you forget?

There was only a trickle of kids going through the gates now and right at the end of that trickle was another face I recognised. One that hadn't changed a bit. Toby Mitten. Skinny, spotty, runty Toby Mitten. Trust him to be the last out of school on a Friday.

I nudged Phil's arm. 'Shall we?'

He looked blank. 'What?'

'Toby Mitten. You wouldn't believe how much I've missed punching him. I reckon I've got withdrawal symptoms.'

But Phil shook his head. 'Don't.'

Toby had seen us and slowed. He'd rather get soaked in the rain than have to walk past us. And that made me feel good. He remembered me all right.

But Phil waved him over. 'Toby hangs around with me these days.'

I looked at him, wanting to see him grin or wink or even being sarcastic. I would have grinned or winked back.

Toby Mitten came right over to us. 'Hi,' he said to me. 'Long time no see.' He said it right to me. 'How're you doing?' He even held his hand out for me to shake.

I was massively offended. Who did he think he was? I wanted to punch the Long time how're you doing? right off his stupid face. But Phil grabbed my arm.

'Hey! What?'

'We're mates,' Phil said.

I don't think I'd have been more surprised if Mickey Thomas had flown out of the sky riding on his favourite tractor. 'But he's Toby Mitten,' I said. I tried to pull my arm out of Phil's grip.

He wouldn't let me go. 'We're mates,' he repeated.

I don't think I'd have been more hurt if Mickey had landed his tractor right on top of me. 'But we're mates. Kenzie, Phil and Panny. *Brook Crooks*, right? Remember?'

Phil let go of me, rolled his eyes. 'Brook Crooks sounded lame even when we were twelve.'

I stood there. Just stood there. I stood there and didn't know what to say.

Phil said, 'Toby helps me with my homework. How else am I going to get away from here? You're lucky. Don't think I'm planning on staying in this hole forever either.'

I stood there getting wet. But getting angry too. Because I couldn't understand what was happening. Two years I'd spent in a middle of nowhere place that I hated, wanting to come back here. Two years I'd wanted my old life back. I'd full-on loved everything about Brook. But everything had changed, and I just couldn't get my head around why. I was getting hot right behind my eyes.

Weird thin-Phil said, 'Maybe Toby can do that *Xbox* day with us. That'd be a laugh, right? I'm sure Panny'd –'

It was too much. Way too much. I spun on Toby. All my anger volcanoed up in me. I lashed out, swung for him.

But he was quicker than me. I felt his fist before I saw it. I felt it a lot. And I fell back onto my arse.

Phil jumped in between us, almost as if he was trying to stop Toby from punching me again. Which was bizarre. I was sure it should be the other way around. But my nose throbbed and the puddle I was sitting in just made me feel cold and stupid and I wasn't in the mood to hit anyone anymore. So I just sat there.

'What's wrong with you?' Phil looked at me like I was the weird one. 'Get a grip, can't you? Grow up or something. Maybe you're the big man at your new school with your big new mate, but not here.'

I couldn't tell him the truth about Mickey Thomas. I might have done, but not in front of Toby Mitten. So I just sat there.

'Come on, Toby.' And with a final look of disgust weird thin-Phil walked away.

But Toby said to me, 'We're going round my house, if you want to come with us.'

'Piss off.'

'Just leave him,' Phil shouted. And they did.

When they'd gone I stood up again. I touched my nose – winced. I was alone at the gates now, everybody else had gone home. I looked at Brook's grey blocks of classrooms and science labs, the drama hall, the library, the gym. They looked the same. I'd thought I knew them all so well, but… But now I reckoned this was an even worse weird upside-down elsewhere kind of place than my new school.

I had a big, thick pen in my pocket. I wrote '*Kenzie woz ere*' on the nearest gatepost, but put the date from two years ago. I hoped the rain wouldn't wash it away.

ARCHIPELAGO

by MARCUS SEDGWICK

In the small cluster of islands that lie between North Uist and Harris is one, just 500 metres at its widest point, less than three times that in length. As far as anyone has found out, there was never a Gaelic name for the island; when Victorian tourists began to explore the area, it was given, unofficially, the only name it's ever had – Elsewhere. Elsewhere is shaped like an exclamation mark; a narrow isthmus connects the dot at the bottom to the bulk of the island, the permanent population of which is one. The crofter who lives there used to rent an old croft house to holidaymakers, outward bound groups and the like, but not any more. In August 1995 a teenage boy went missing while on a holiday for underprivileged city children. No one has stayed on the island since. This is a fictionalised account of what happened that summer.

NICK SHOOES THE teenagers into the kitchen. Naomi finishes up with Aonghas, the apparently ancient crofter who's rented the old croft house for a song. The charity they work for has a tight budget and it's cost a fortune to get the eight of them to the island; a cheap house was just what they needed.

Aonghas, while not exactly the epitome of warmth, is a reasonable enough man to deal with, and the rent, though small, is probably enough of an incentive to him to make visitors feel welcome and comfortable, though the place is far from luxurious, a fact not lost on the kids.

The six of them, the three girls, the three boys, stand staring at the floor rather than each other. It's late, they're tired. The girls are playing with a couple of cats that seem to come with the house. The boys sit at the large kitchen table, their bags still around them on the floor.

Nick looks at the children, not for the first time wondering if his work is as valuable as he likes to think it is. He and Naomi have both been at the charity for five years, long enough for the zeal to start waning, though certainly not long enough for them to have become embittered.

But trips like this, that take forever to organise, to bring just six young people all the way from London to this remote place, and... for what? He knows what it says on the charity's mission statement, and if provoked would get angry defending the work they did, but really, would it 'fundamentally change' the lives of the kids to spend a week on a remote Scottish island? Would it 'empower' them? Would it 'develop' them? Or would it just bore them to death?

As Naomi joins them, she shuts the door behind her with a sigh.

'I'm bushed. Tea?'

Niall, as usual, is the first to talk.

'Maybe it's like the kangaroo,' he says, in that quick, clipped way he has. The oldest of the boys, fourteen, yet probably the least mature. His life is lived through books and films, and any understanding he has of the serious things in life is derived from these.

Becca is not too tired to enjoy one of Niall's escapades.

'The kangaroo?' she laughs, leaving the cats.

'Yes,' Niall explains. 'The island. It doesn't have a name, that's what Nick said, isn't it, Nick? Not a Gaelic name, just Elsewhere, which is a pretty stupid name for any place, but maybe it's like the kangaroo. You know, when white people settled in Australia and they saw this big thing bouncing about, like a bunny, but twenty times as big, and they asked a local, you know, an aborigine, and said, "what's that?" and the aborigine said, "kangaroo", which just means "I don't know".'

Becca laughs again.

'That's not true.'

'It is,' Niall says, not at all offended. 'Nick, that's true isn't it? So maybe it's the same here. Maybe someone came to the mainland near here and said, "What's that place called?" and the local said "Oh, that's not here. That's just somewhere else. Elsewhere."'

Nick smiles.

'An interesting theory,' he says. No one else looks interested. 'But do you know what is true? The island doesn't appear on any maps.'

Dylan and even quiet little Robbie look up now.

'Are you going to tell us a spooky story?' smiles Naomi. 'Maybe tomorrow night, when we're not so tired.'

Nick holds up a hand, shrugs.

'No ghost story. It's true. There was some old fuss about this place. Private land, some ancestors of Aonghas' maybe, went to a lot of trouble to stop the old Ordnance Survey from surveying. Said it was modern nonsense, they could see one end of the island from the other, so why did they need to draw it?'

'I don't see what cats are for.'

Niall again. No one is surprised by this kind of thing now, not after three days from London to get here in a small minibus and a boat from the mainland.

'What's that, Niall?'

'Dogs I get,' he says. 'I can see the point of dogs. You can have a conversation with a dog.'

'You could have a conversation with a wall,' says Becca.

'Yes, well, possibly I could, but I would prefer to talk to a wall than to a cat. They just sit there, looking at you. Then they want food. You feed them. You wait a few hours, during which they look at you again. Or sleep. I mean, what's the point?'

Ruby, the cool girl, shakes her head.

'You are seriously weird, Niall.'

'Hey,' says Nick, warningly, but Niall, as usual, either doesn't hear or doesn't care.

'I mean, look at that one.'

He nods at the black cat, which had hopped up onto the shelf above the range, where it sat, glaring at them.

'I mean, that is, at best, one very sulky beast and, at worst, some cohort of the devil!'

'What's a cohort?' asks Dylan.

'Associate. Business partner. Partner in crime. Friend. Chum,' says Nick. 'That kind of thing.'

'So why can't you just say friend, Niall?' asks Dylan.

'Not as much fun to say that. Cohort is more fun. Cohort. Try it.'

Dylan does.

'Cohort,' he says, thoughtfully. He smiles. 'Yeah you're right. Cohort. Cohort. Cohort, cohort, cohort.'

Then they're all saying it, even Ruby, and Nick and Naomi exchange a weary but happy glance, and send them all to unpack.

After food, the boys one by one slope off to bed, then the girls decide to go at the same time, and Nick and Naomi sit by the open fire, trying to get the coal to burn a bit better.

'I think this might be all right,' Nick says.

'Wait till day three before you say that. No TV, no video games. Half of them don't read. The island is smaller than most shopping centres, and with much less to do unless you like sheep. And as you well know these are all kids with serious problems.'

'Is it actually August here, by the way? It's freezing.' He pokes the fire again. 'I know they have problems, but we've coped with worse. Remember Portugal?'

There's a slight pause, and Nick realises she might be thinking about what else happened in Portugal, besides them empowering some really mixed-up kids. Or rather, what almost happened between them.

'Okay, so let's just say that my jury is out. Let's see how tomorrow goes. This is going to stretch even our amazing skills.'

'We'll break them in gently,' Nick says. 'Route march round the perimeter of the island, build a fort from sheep's droppings before lunch. So forth.'

'Deal,' said Naomi, smiling. 'But take it easy on them, yes? I'm not sure how much of an outdoors man Niall is, for example.'

Nick feigns outrage.

'What are you suggesting?'

'Well, what I'm *suggesting*,' Naomi says, 'is that the boy is *completely* gay. He just doesn't know it yet.'

'How very inclusive of you. Just because he is precise and tidy and funny and...'

'It's not a criticism to say he's gay,' Naomi says. 'You're the one with the issues if you think it's a criticism.'

'You win. What about the others? Would you like to stereotype them too, while you're about it?'

'Fine. Ruby, cool chick. Missing her boyfriend. Very serious thing at fourteen you know. Clary, hippy parents. Bet you anything. Becca, arty parents. Too bright for her own good.'

'That's a really...'

'I mean it. I know the type. Niall, well, you have my views. Dylan, funny, the joker, but I think he's pretty practical too. Did you see how he helped with the bags? I didn't even have to ask and there he was. Robbie, well, Robbie... Robbie's a bit harder. He's so quiet. I mean SO quiet.'

Nick is suddenly thoughtful. Quiet.

'Well, given the levels of abuse he's had, maybe that's hardly surprising. If we can even get a smile out of him, I'll call this week a success.'

'Agreed. They're the usual odd bunch, aren't they? Proving once again that dysfunctionality comes in all shapes and sizes. You'd be hard pressed to guess there was anything wrong with Becca, for example. Three suicide attempts at thirteen. That's pretty hardcore.'

The two of them fall silent.

The fire dies. They are cold and they move closer to each other. Nick puts an arm round Naomi.

'It's not that cold,' she says.

He takes his arm away again, and they turn in.

The following day is bright, sunny, and warm.

The eight stand outside the croft house, staring open-mouthed at the endless sea in front of them.

'We are but a speck,' says Niall, very quietly, after a very long time.

No one disagrees. They all understand him for once. The island, *their* island for the week, is just a sliver of earth floating in a universe of water.

'Is that Shakespeare, Niall?' asks Naomi.

The boy grins.

'Glad you think so. Pure Niall Marshall.'

They stand a while longer.

'Right,' says Nick, eventually, but brightly. 'Let's explore.'

They do, with varying degrees of enthusiasm.

Niall hangs out with the 'grown-ups', as he likes to call Nick and Naomi. Dylan and Robbie and Becca come along next. Ruby and Clary are the most reluctant, dragging along at the back, though not unhappily. They are talking about boys, and by boys they do not mean Niall or Dylan or Robbie.

They spend an hour or two on the shoreline, not doing very much, not feeling the need to do very much, and just before they decide to head for home, they see the dot of the exclamation mark, at the far south of the island. A narrow strip of shingle is all that connects the dot to the 'mainland' and it's easy to see that the shingle would disappear during any half-decent storm.

'Wow,' says Dylan, 'look at that.'

He points up onto the hill of the dot, where he's seen what no one else has yet, an ancient circle of stones, long craggy fingers pointing at the sky.

'Can we go there?' he asks Nick.

Nick nods.

'Absolutely. After lunch. Come on.'

They return to the dot, crossing the narrow shingle isthmus in single file, and spend a long time walking round the eight stones, peering at them, touching them, leaning against them, hiding behind them.

It's about half an hour before Clary, of all people, says, 'You know, this would be a really cool place to camp. The night. Nick, you did say we could camp out one night.'

'I said maybe we could. We have no tents. It would have to be a still night.'

'But we could have a big campfire and cook food on it and bring our sleeping bags.'

Clary's enthusiasm for camping is surprising and infectious.

Everyone agrees it sounds fun, even Ruby.

As they make their way back to the house, Naomi winks at Nick.

'See. Hippy parents. That's another fiver you owe me.'

Nick points out they hadn't actually made a bet.

'Well, I bet you a fiver they don't all last the night.'

'What, you think we're actually going to do it?'

'Sure. Why not? We should encourage any initiative, right?'

Nick smiles.

'Fair enough. The first still night, then.'

A still night does not come to begin with.

There are two nights that are anything but calm. On the first, Becca wakes up the whole house with a screaming fit in the small hours.

She will talk to no one, explain nothing, and in the end Naomi sits with her downstairs on the sofa till she finally falls asleep as the sun starts to edge over the mountains away on the mainland.

The next night, Dylan is violently sick; it turns out he's allergic to red pepper, and just forgot to tell anyone. The soup was tomato and peppers.

So, on the fourth night after their arrival, they venture down to the dot. They have spent all day preparing. There are no trees on the island, but they've found a pile of smashed-up pallets in a shed that they can use as firewood for a campfire. Nick, Dylan, Robbie and Becca have spent all afternoon carrying the wood down, in four or five trips. Naomi, Clary, Ruby and Niall have been making food that will be easy to cook on the campfire: potatoes in tinfoil, sausages and beans.

'That's what I like about camp cooking,' says Niall, 'no vegetables.'

Naomi wonders exactly how much camping he's ever done. She knows about his life, his problems. How he can pretend to be so breezy about things brings a lump to her throat. But then, that's often what these kids are like. The desire to live eventually breaks through the hard stuff. Sometimes.

Now, they make their way down to the stone circle, carrying their sleeping bags.

The sun is starting to dip into the sea; it's a perfectly calm and still evening.

They stand for a moment, before Nick announces that they should get the fire going. They do. It's easy – the wood is old and has been sitting in the shed behind the house for who knows how long.

Soon they are toasting their toes, eating from tins, waiting for the potatoes to be done.

It's Niall who says, 'Eight.'

'What now?' laughs Becca.

'Eight stones! Eight of us. One each. That's good, because we don't have to squabble.'

'Squabble?'

'Well, supposing there were nine of us. We'd have to play musical chairs.'

'Let's all choose a stone,' says Clary.

When the potatoes are ready, they all get one and take it back to their chosen stone.

'Who do you suppose made this place?' asks Robbie, so quietly that no one can believe he has spoken. No one answers, because no one knows.

The night deepens, and though it is still, it gets cold. The fire flickers.

Nick wanders over to it and stirs it, throwing some more old pallet wood on.

He returns, not to his stone, but to Naomi's. He sits down beside her. The kids are chatting, quietly, all seeming quite calm.

'I think I might win that fiver,' says Nick.

Naomi laughs gently and they sit staring at the flames for a long time.

'Is it cold enough?' says Nick, faintly.

Naomi understands.

'Almost,' she says, slyly. 'Al-most.'

They whisper to each other, heedless of other whispering, whispering in the water, a short stone's throw from where they huddle.

'I think it is going to be all right,' says Naomi. 'You were right.'

Nick smiles in the darkness.

Suddenly, like a dream descending, it is quiet.

No one speaks.

Becca shrieks. Just once, and then is still. Everyone looks at her to see what is wrong; her eyes are wide and she is pointing at Niall, or rather, just over his shoulder.

Her lips move, but no sound comes out.

Every eye turns to where she is pointing, all except Niall, who is frozen, infected by the fear on Becca's face.

What the others see is another face, but it is not human, not exactly. In the darkness, the half-light of the fire, they can see a face that appears to hover just behind Niall. The skin of the face is dark blue, and glistens in the light. It is wet, as if it has slipped up and out of the ocean just behind them, and crawled to the circle. Its head is bald, its shoulders are naked, the rest of it is lost in shadow.

The skin is blue, the eyes are black, just empty black pits.

'Niall,' hisses Nick. 'Don't move.'

Niall raises his hand too, points at Nick.

'There's one behind you, too.'

And then they realise that there is one of the strange faces just behind each of them. The faces are expressionless, unreadable. They show neither hostility nor anger, fear nor kindness.

Blue skin, black eyes.

And then they slip away into the darkness, and it is only after they have retreated that Becca starts to scream.

'It's okay, it's okay,' shouts Nick, running to her, 'they've gone. Whatever they were, they've gone.'

But Becca has seen what no one else has.

'But so has Robbie. Robbie's gone. He's gone. They've taken him.'

All eyes turn to the stone where little quiet Robbie had sat, eating his potato.

They search for hours in the dark, and the next day too when daylight comes, until the police arrive.

They do not find him.

His empty sleeping bag lies on the ground, a mundane memorial for a troubled boy.

THE UNCLAIMED GIRL

by BARRY HUTCHISON

IMELDA BROWN STOOD on the platform, wondering what the hell was going on. She had just stepped off a train, which was confusing, as she had no memory of stepping on one.

Behind her, other passengers disembarked. They milled around on the platform, eyeing each other suspiciously, all looking just as bewildered as Imelda felt. A bright blue, cloudless sky hung overhead. This was also causing Imelda concern. Last time she'd checked it had been snowing, and it had been cold, and it had been dark.

A man, grey hair and wrinkles, grabbed her by her coat sleeve. Instinctively, Imelda yanked her arm away, but the man barely seemed to notice.

'W-where am I?' he asked, his voice cracking. 'Where is this?'

Imelda glanced around. A large, impressive building, all sand-stone pillars and tall, arched windows, boxed them in on three sides.

There appeared to be just one platform – the one they were standing on. The word 'ARRIVALS' was printed on a billboard hung above the tracks. She couldn't see a sign for departures, and there was nothing to reveal the station's name.

'No idea,' Imelda admitted.

'I can't find Dorothy,' the man fretted. 'I can't find my Dotty. Have you seen her?'

Imelda shook her head. 'No,' she said. 'Sorry.'

Wringing his hands, the man turned and stumbled through the crowd, calling out Dotty's name.

For the first time, Imelda looked properly at her fellow passengers. There were a hundred or more of them, all looking lost. Most of those she could see appeared to be in their late sixties or older, but there were a few forty-somethings in the mix, too. No one her age, though. Not even close.

A few people were talking, but from their body language it was clear none of them was listening to what the others were saying. Some of the older ones were crying. Some of the younger ones too. Imelda shook her head. Crying never got anyone anywhere.

A loud musical note rang out, silencing the rising hysteria before it could fully build. Imelda looked in the direction of the sound. A uniformed man stood farther along the platform, blowing into a battered old trumpet.

The note lasted for several seconds. When it had finished, the man brought the instrument down sharply to his side and cast his gaze across the now silent occupants of the platform.

His uniform was a navy blue coat over a matching waistcoat and trousers. Brass buttons, polished to a brilliant sheen, stood out against the dark material. On his head was a cap with an official-looking badge sewn to the front of it. Imelda was too far away to read what the badge said, but she guessed it was something to do with the railway. He wasn't police anyway. She could tell one of them a mile off.

The man noisily cleared his throat, patted down his thick moustache, and began to speak.

'Ladies and gentlemen, I am the Station Master,' he said in a voice that did nothing to set Imelda at ease. It was an officious, self-important voice. She'd heard plenty like it before, and hated every one. 'In a calm, orderly fashion you will all follow me. Stay close together, no wandering off.'

'What's going on?' called someone from the crowd. 'Where are we?'

'All in good time,' replied the Station Master. He performed a stiff about-turn and began marching in the direction of a door marked 'EXIT'. 'Now come along,' he ordered. 'I can't be standing around here all day.'

A low muttering spread through the crowd. Slowly, though, everyone began to follow the Station Master towards the door. Imelda hung back, waiting until most of the throng had passed through the exit before following.

She heard the first cry of shock just as she reached the door. She tried to retreat, but the people behind her kept pushing forward, carrying her on through.

'Get off,' she snapped. 'Stop pushing.'

More yells and screams from up ahead drowned her out. She stumbled through the doorway, her eyes frantically scanning for another exit, for some way to escape whatever was happening to her fellow passengers.

It was only as she was shoved in amongst the shouts and the squeals that she realised they were cries of delight, not fear. Dozens – in fact *hundreds* – of people stood just beyond a row of polished chrome turnstiles. Men and women of every age and race huddled together, grinning and cheering excitedly as the passengers entered from the platform.

'Mum?' squawked a middle-aged woman on the other side of the turnstiles.

An old woman at Imelda's side turned her head sharply at the sound of her daughter's voice. 'B-Becca?' she gasped. Her hand flew to her mouth and tears sprang to her eyes. Imelda moved aside to let her pass, but the Station Master stepped into her path, hand raised.

'Not yet,' he said, stopping the woman in her tracks. He gave his moustache another pat and adjusted his hat before continuing. 'This is Station Sixty-Two. Beyond the gates you will find people waiting for you. Some of them you may know, many of them you will not. Those you do not know will have signs. If you see your name on a sign, go to that person and they will take care of you until you are in a position to take care of yourself.'

The Station Master carried on talking, but Imelda had stopped listening. She was scanning the waiting crowd, searching for a face she recognised, but finding none.

About a quarter of those waiting clutched home-made signs. Silently, she read off the names. *Ameena Ahmed. Maggie Cooper. Yan-Yan Chow.* There were others, many others. But no *Imelda Brown.*

'Right then,' barked the Station Master, finally stepping aside. 'On your way, the lot of you.'

Like crashing waves, large sections of the crowd surged forward. They called and gestured to those waiting for them, falling over one another as they fought their way through the turnstiles.

Imelda watched them. She watched the hugging, the kissing, the handshaking. She heard the chatter and the laughter and the tears. And she wished, for a moment, that she were part of it.

But she wasn't. And that was that.

Less than twenty passengers remained on her side of the turnstiles. One by one they spotted their names. One by one they approached those holding 'their' sign. Polite smiles and introductions were exchanged. Questions were asked, and answers given, but Imelda was too far away to hear.

In dribs and drabs the passengers and their new-found companions filed away. Imelda stood her ground, watching them until there was no-one left but her.

'Okay,' she muttered, although she wasn't quite sure why. She blew out her cheeks and shook her head. 'Okay.'

'Why are you still here?' demanded the Station Master. Imelda jumped. She'd forgotten he was even there.

'Um… Hi. I don't know where – '

The man jabbed a thumb in the direction of a desk, way against the far wall. 'Unclaimed Girls,' he snapped.

Imelda blinked. 'What?'

'You deaf? *Unclaimed Girls*. Go,' he said. 'There,' he said. '*Now.*'

Imelda felt her fists clench. The temptation to punch the Station Master right in his scowling face was great, but she knew that hitting someone in uniform was never a good idea. Not from the front, anyway.

Biting her lip, she pushed through the closest turnstile. The station building was as impressive inside as it was outside – a vast, cathedral-like construction with enormous pillars stretching all the way up to the high, domed ceiling. The thud of her boots on the polished floor echoed around the now-empty station as she made her way over to the desk. It was a flimsy, flat-packed bit of furniture, stained with coffee rings and blue biro – an obvious afterthought among the grandeur of the station.

A pudgy, red-haired woman slumped behind the desk, a cigarette hanging from her bottom lip. As Imelda approached, a blob of ash fell from the end of the woman's cigarette and vanished into her impressive cleavage. She seemed neither to notice nor care.

'Yes?' the woman asked.

'Hi,' Imelda began. 'Is this… UNCLAIMED GIRLS?'

The woman took the cigarette from her mouth, blew a smoke ring, then inhaled it back up through her nose. She tapped a small wooden sign on the desktop. 'That's what it says.'

Imelda's eye twitched. 'So it does.' She watched the woman take another long draw of the cigarette. 'Those things'll kill you. You know that?'

The woman's expression didn't change. 'Funny,' she said, after a long pause. 'Now, what do you want?'

Imelda leaned over the desk. 'Answers,' she said. 'Like where I am. And how I got here.' She picked up the 'UNCLAIMED GIRLS' sign. 'And what this means.'

A sheet of paper was slid across the desk towards her. Imelda glanced down at it. 'What's this?'

'Registration document B7784,' the woman said, stubbing out one cigarette and lighting another. 'Fill it in.'

Imelda scanned the document. It was a questionnaire. Name. Date of birth. Marital status. The usual. The fourth question jumped out at her though. She had to read it three times before she was satisfied she'd read it correctly.

'What does this one mean?' she asked, tapping the page.

The woman didn't look down. 'Pretty self-explanatory, I'd have thought.'

'Aye, but... Is it a joke?'

'Do I look like I'm laughing?'

Imelda turned back to the paper. She read the question again. It was simple enough. Just three words. She read them once more, out loud this time.

'*Cause of Death?*'

Across the desk, the woman gave a theatrical sigh. 'Look,' she said, 'I'll make it easy. How old are you?'

'What?' Imelda said, dragging her eyes away from the page. 'Fifteen.'

'Too young for Ratched's, too old for Nessie's,' the woman muttered. 'Teeth.'

Imelda frowned. 'Teeth?'

'Teeth. Show me.' The woman chomped the air a few times to demonstrate.

Caught off guard, Imelda pulled a grimace, showing her teeth and gums.

'Seen worse, but Hawthorne won't take you.'

A commotion behind her made Imelda turn around. People were filing into the station. They hurried over to the turnstiles and stood there, waiting impatiently for the platform door to open.

'I haven't got time for this,' the woman sighed. She pushed aside an overflowing ashtray, revealing a small intercom built into the desk top. There was a loud *buzz* as she pressed a button. 'We'll go with Windsome. You're about the right age.'

'Right age for what?' Imelda asked.

'Hello?' said a woman's voice over the intercom. 'Miss Windsome speaking.'

'Yeah, hello, Miss Windsome. It's Jane at the desk. We've got one for you.'

'Really? Thank you, Jane,' trilled the voice. 'I shall be right with you.'

Click. Jane released the intercom button and leaned back in her chair. 'She'll be right with you. Take a seat.'

'Who'll be right with me?' Imelda demanded. 'What's going on?'

'Take a seat,' Jane repeated.

Imelda slammed her hands down on the desk. 'If you don't tell me what the hell's going on, I swear I'm going to make you eat that cigarette.'

'Hello, dear,' called a voice from right behind her. Imelda

turned and found herself face to face with a grey-haired woman in an enormous brute of a dress. It was shiny and satiny, all puffed out from the waist like a giant lampshade. A flowery bonnet completed the look.

'Jesus,' Imelda muttered, looking the woman up and down. 'I didn't realise it was fancy dress.'

'I'm Miss Windsome,' the woman said, ignoring the jibe. 'Headmistress of Miss Windsome's School for Unclaimed Girls. I suspect you have many questions.'

'Aye,' Imelda said. '*Starting with where am I?*'

'Dead. I'm afraid you're dead,' Miss Windsome smiled apologetically. 'Sorry.'

Imelda didn't bother to argue. There was no reason to. Somehow, she knew the woman was telling the truth.

'I'm... I'm...'

A bubble rose up in her stomach. It was in her throat before she knew it, threatening to emerge as a scream of panic, but she swallowed it back down and gave herself a shake. Panic was pointless, and she'd learned long ago that nobody came when she screamed.

It was over. Her life was over. She'd just have to accept that and move on.

'Dead. Right.' She jabbed a thumb in Jane's direction. 'I'm guessing by the look on her coupon that I'm not in Heaven.'

'I heard that.'

Miss Windsome shook her head. 'No, not Heaven, but not... not the other place, either. It turned out we were a bit off the mark on those fronts. There's only here.'

'The railway station?'

'The City.'

Imelda looked to the station's main doors. 'A city?'

'*The City*,' Miss Windsome corrected. 'The City of the Dead.' She gave a polite cough. 'How did you…? If you don't mind me asking?' She paused, composing herself. 'What's the last thing you remember?'

'Cold,' Imelda said, quietly. She remembered the frost biting at her fingers and toes, the icy kiss of the concrete step beneath her, the uncontrollable shakes as the snow came down and down and down, covering her like a shroud. 'I… I was cold. Lying in the snow.'

'You were lying in the snow? *Outside*? Why?'

'There was nowhere else to go.'

'Why on earth didn't you go home?'

Imelda saw her breath cloud in front of her face, felt wetness trickle down her cheek. She moved quickly, wiping the tear with the back of her hand. But she didn't move quickly enough.

'Oh!' said Miss Windsome, her voice cracking. 'Oh, you poor dear.'

Imelda turned on her. 'Don't say that,' she growled. 'Don't call me that!'

'Oh, but you are,' Miss Windsome insisted. 'It's terrible, you poor dear.'

'Quit it. I'm not a poor dear. I'm not a poor *anything*, alright? When are you people going to get that through your thick skulls?'

Miss Windsome blinked. 'You people?'

'Do-gooders,' Imelda snapped. 'Busybodies. Social work-ers. Whatever. You're all the same. It's all '*poor dear, must be so* hungry' and 'poor dear, must be so scared' and 'poor dear, isn't it terrible?' Talking about me like I'm just a thing to be pitied.'

She took a deep breath, held it, then let it out. When she spoke again, some of the harshness had left her voice. 'I don't want pity.'

Miss Windsome nodded. 'Very well,' she said. 'But outside this station, beyond those doors, walks everyone who has ever died. Victorians. Romans. Aztecs. Modern-agers, like you. Everyone.'

'Everyone? That'd be hundreds of billions of people.'

'Well,' said Miss Windsome, smoothing the front of her dress, 'I wouldn't know about that. But I do know that at my school you would be kept safe from the many dangers out there on those streets.'

She stepped closer. 'You would be fed. You would be educated. You would be given something to replace those *awful* clothes.'

Imelda looked down at what she was wearing. Her heavy boots and dark, dirty denim were a stark contrast to the headmistress's outfit. 'What's wrong with my clothes?'

Behind her desk, Jane snorted out a laugh, then lit another cigarette.

'There are other girls, too,' Miss Windsome continued, 'your age. Friends, perhaps.'

'I can survive on my own,' Imelda said.

The headmistress gestured around them. 'Perhaps not the best choice of word, given the circumstances?'

Imelda didn't answer. She could hear sounds now from outside. Car engines. Voices. City sounds.

Miss Windsome reached out and smiled warmly. Imelda looked at the offered hand and felt her own twitch in response. Her eyes met those of the headmistress. 'I could really get that stuff?' she asked. 'That stuff you said?'

Miss Windsome nodded. 'Food, clothes, education, companionship. It would all be yours.' She gave a slight shrug of her shoulders. 'I'll be honest, you're not what we'd usually look for in a Windsome Girl, but we could make an exception.'

Imelda's hand went limp.

'Why would you do that?'

'Well... given the circumstances.'

'What circumstances?'

'You know,' began Miss Windsome, 'with you being...'

Imelda said the words for her, but the frosty edge had left her voice. 'A poor dear. Right.'

'I didn't mean it like that.'

Imelda shrugged. 'Yes, you did.'

She turned away from the headmistress and looked towards the main door. There was a city out there.

'I'm dead,' she said. 'I'm really dead.'

Miss Windsome nodded. 'Yes you are. We have counsellors to help you come to terms with that.'

'Forget it,' Imelda said. She looked through the windows at the brilliant blue sky. It looked nicer than snow, any day. Warmer, too. 'I think I already have.'

A city. Not hers, maybe, but a city all the same. She took a step towards the door.

'What are you doing?' Miss Windsome gasped. 'It's dangerous out there. There are... there are... *Vikings*!'

Imelda paused. 'Vikings? What, like actual proper Vikings?'

'Yes! Real Vikings!'

'Cool.'

Miss Windsome shook her head. 'No! They're dangerous. The whole city is dangerous. A girl couldn't possibly cope on her own!'

Imelda smiled. Her first real smile in as far back as she could remember. 'Come on,' she said, 'I'm dead. What's the worst that can happen?'

Feeling more alive than she ever had, Imelda Brown ran across the station, past the waiting crowds, and hauled open the door. The warmth of the sun prickled her skin as she slipped into the hustle and bustle of the City of the Dead.

Still unclaimed.

THE THINGS I BROUGHT WITH ME WHEN I KNEW WE WERE LEAVING HOME FOREVER

by JENNY VALENTINE

M Y GRANDMOTHER WAS the thinnest woman I ever knew. Her ankles stuck like reeds from the dark, weighted pools of her shoes. Her wrists, busy and snappable and determined, drowned in their sleeves. Her clothes always billowed, hitched up and cinched in with string and extra stitches.

She might actually have fit in my suitcase, if we'd had time.

She was so light and so quick, when I was little I thought the wind might pick her up and take her, but it never did, and just by being there, just by existing, she made a place safe.

I thought so anyway. For a long time that's what I thought.

We spent our days together. Her spidery, gaunt hands taught me how to make bread, how to hold a chicken so it hangs from your grip, dazed and expectant, how to steam the stamp from a

85

letter and use it again, how to plant anything and make it grow.

I can see her now. I step in from the sun through her shadowed doorway, her house the only still thing in a tornado, the only thing that's stayed the same. There's the low tick of a clock, and the family portraits, the smell of something stewing, the shabby old lace tablecloth she made before she married, used and re-used, the dark quiet. And outside in the yard, there she is, shooing the chickens, planting marigolds while the war rains down around her.

When the men came, she tried not to let them in. The first one struck at her as she spoke and she flew like a feather in the air, slowed down almost, drifting, and then all of a sudden landing in the corner with her legs bent under her and her hands up to meet the wall.

I'd never seen my grandmother fall before.

They swarmed through the house like locusts. It shrank around them, up-ended, stripped dry. They trampled on soil, and paper faces and broken glass.

'They're not here,' she said from her corner, like they were looking for my parents in the cups and books, in the split and bleeding cushions.

'They're not here,' she said again, louder, her teeth framed in blood, her tongue thickened with it.

The wrong kind of blood, apparently. The wrong breed.

All I did was scream.

My grandmother reminds me of that now. She sits at her window with her sewing and she looks at me over her glasses.

'The noise you made,' she says, shaking her head, her mouth stuck with pins. 'Like cats.'

'Sorry, Nana,' I tell her, and she smiles, and the pins glint.

It was her money that paid for us to leave. She counted it out, the notes falling from her hands so we had to bend and scrabble for them in the dust. More money than I had ever seen, hidden in her shoes, stitched into the fabric of her clothes, buried in her garden. She wouldn't come with us. She laughed and shook her head when I asked her. She turned her back to me before I had finished waving.

It is dark in the hut at night.

Not dark like when we came here, pindrop-quiet in the back of the lorry, scared to breathe. It was so airless then, and so utterly, solidly black that after a while I began to wonder if there was such a thing as light, or if I'd only dreamt it. Not dark like it was then, because nothing is, but dark so you can't see your hand in front of your face, so you can't see what it's doing.

It is too noisy to sleep. I don't know how they all do it. The wind sprints at us across the flat of the fields and tries to climb in through all the gaps and slits and spaces at once, complaining if it doesn't, howling with the effort of going round.

My father snores, the cavern of his throat collapsed, his breathing loud and liquid. I think this is what he has yearned for all day long, this oblivion.

My father drinks to forget. He drinks because there is no longer a good reason to have a steady hand. Because we ran away and left his mother at home and, unlike me, he cannot see her. Because we ran away to this. How do you shave with a rusted up razor and five families queuing to use the same tap? How do you maintain your standards? How does a Professor find better work than picking potatoes? My father drinks because the life he had is over.

Who can blame him?

My mother is quiet when she sleeps, but before she sleeps she prays. Not so I can hear the words she offers up to God (whose fault it is, I say, that we are here) but just so I can hear the soft plump and click of her speaking, the movements her mouth makes while she gives thanks for whatever it is we are left with. The sound of her is pretty, I listen for it in the dark, but sometimes I think my mother is a fool.

It is not until everyone else is asleep, and my mother is quiet, and my father is snoring, and I am left with only the wind for company, that I fumble for the suitcase hidden under my bed and open it.

Out she climbs, my grandmother, with the sun on her sunken, appled skin, and her chickens swaggering after her, and her bread-stick limbs.

She brings me the things I asked for.

A jar of light.

The light from home, that splices instantly into planes of sun and shade; the light that warms your skin, first thing and all day;

the light that bathes all it touches in clean gold.

I've remembered this light and longed for it. Here, the light is weak and grey and falls flat and uniform and there is no heat in it. It is like the pause before sunrise, but sunrise never comes. It is a constant waiting.

My grandmother opens the jar for me, smiling, and the air fills with hot gold and the red of the dust in her yard, and a sharp marigold orange. This black hut seethes with colour. For a moment I see the true green of my blanket, my arms a living brown, the veins beneath the skin bright blue. Like striking a match, until she puts the lid back, so as not to waste it, or wake the others. It snaps out, and is dark again, with the wind screaming, and just a faint glow to see things by.

My book of plants.

The book we made together, my grandmother and I, fat with seeds and pressed flowers and my slow, painstaking handwriting, her deft drawings of leaves. The book that contains her whole garden, all its secrets, and the things I know are true because she told me. It's heavier than I remember when she gives it to me, thick and powdery with damp, the binding come loose, creased and muddied by the boots of soldiers. Our book garden crouches beneath my fingers, poised, impatient to begin. I turn the pages and they sigh and crump like moths' wings, beating against my hands.

How to take a cutting from a rose and make a new one. How to marry two trees. How to grow tomatoes with skins like water.

How to entice bees. How to make medicines from every flower. How to store a seed so even after generations of quiet dryness, it will grow.

While I am reading our garden, I hear it, her red and silver radio.

From the shelf in my grandmother's kitchen, with a broken handle and a dial that leaps and crackles when it turns. She holds it to my ear, its song scratched and faint, with a buzz like constant applause, like a standing ovation. I clap too at the rare sound of it, my mother tongue, so nonchalant, so everyday. And beneath it, I hear the growl of traffic and car horns, a chorus of birds and dogs and voices, of clattering wheels and hurrying feet, the sounds of home.

My mother shifts and turns in her sleep and I look up and then the purring starts, the honeyed rumble of our cat, stretching in the suitcase like a yogi, blinking, peering out. Not ours, not really, just a tom who liked to stroll in the yard and threaten the chickens, who showed up unannounced at the kitchen window, or curled up on a chair for the afternoon. I hold my hand out to him and he considers it before he gives me his ears to stroke, the weight of his skull pushed firm into my palm, that purr still rolling, that pleasured thrum. I didn't think to ask for him but he came anyway. He stalks the length of my legs, turning, testing the bed for comfort before he curls into my lap, warm and fur-soft and alive.

My grandmother reaches to stroke him and I ask her:

'Anything from Julia?'

She looks away and shakes her head, the lines at her mouth like stitches, sewing it shut.

'Did you give her my letters?'

She nods. Of course she did.

I hand her the latest one, written in my tiniest scrawl on an opened, flattened paper bag.

'Dearest Julia,' it begins, like all the others. 'I hope you are well.'

I am sure she is not.

I think of my best friend, left behind without me. She is on the street where I last saw her, still waving, unable to move because I have frozen her there in time. That way, I am hoping no harm will come to her.

Who am I kidding?

My grandmother stows my letter in the suitcase and I stroke the sleeping cat and we don't talk about Julia as the sky outside starts to lift. The crows on the fields shout down the wind and as beds creak and people shift and wake, she packs the other things too, the jar of light, our garden book, her radio. The cat gets up and climbs in at her gesture. We say goodbye.

It is morning again.

And I am elsewhere, wherever that might be.

WE ARE ALL WAITING

by DENISE MINA

WE ARE VERY angry for the first hour and a half in the queue. We squash up close to one another, mistrustful of our neighbours. They may try to slip in ahead of us if any angle is left uninvigilated. We do not know one another's culture.

In front of me stands a man with a Kenyan passport and small goatie beard. He is tall, a full head taller than the rest of us. Between him and I, standing absurdly close, is a small woman in a blue nylon pashmina. She looks rested. She does not look as if it is five AM and she is in this queue, an angry irksome queue, full of people who have been standing upright for hours, mentally rehearsing the argument we will have with the representative of the airline when it is our turn to be seen.

A rumour starts at the back, a man tells his wife something in what sounds like Tamil: she remonstrates. People translate and the rumour circulates that there is no one at the desk. We are all waiting to get to an empty desk, hoping to be seen by someone who is not there. But we are all too afraid to leave the queue. If we don't wait the person behind us might get our seat on the next plane to where we need to go. The rumour reaches the front and a gentle eyed man shakes his head and gives a little smile, no, there is someone at the desk. They are keeping their head down against this room full of angry, demanding faces.

Still we are not moving.

There is water available. In a passenger lounge around the corner, bottles of water and, bizarrely, individual slices of Dundee cake sealed in plastic. The families are lucky. They can send a member off to get the water and cake, while the single travellers are stranded. We can't even go to the toilet because we will lose our place.

An elderly woman in an airline wheelchair falls asleep. Sad women carry sleeping children, their arms sore, backs aching. Their husbands stare furiously towards the desk, as if through sheer force of will they can conjure a solution.

We can do nothing.

There are six desks on our side of the cavernous white marbled room, an empty corridor fenced by retractable ribbon, and then six desks on the other side with massive queues of their own. Without seeming to move the queues implicate themselves forwards, a millimetre per hour, suspicion and hope propelling us into italics. In the space between the two sides of the room a man in a smart suit directs people back into the queues. Waiting is inevitable.

'This is ridiculous,' announces an American man two queues

away. He goes off to look for a better solution, to threaten and bargain. Fifty minutes later he reappears at the back of the queue. He took a chance and lost his place.

'This is just the worst service I have ever seen.' A man is behind us and announcing this to the crowd. He is from Glasgow, is camp and is absolutely furious. I look around and make the mistake of catching his eye. 'I'm not even going to Brisbane now,' he tells me, 'I'm getting them to transfer my flights and I'm going straight home again.'

I smile inappropriately, pretend that the earphones resting in my ears are on, that I am listening to music and I can't hear him. The skin around his eyes is red because he is so angry. He has a tribal tattoo around his bicep.

'Even the *run up* to this holiday was a disaster.'

I smile again and look away. The small woman in front of me smiles. She is smaller than me, which is very small. She has dusky brown skin and high cheek bones. She is incredibly pretty.

'Were you here long before me?' I ask, hoping she will speak to me and the angry man will catch someone else's eye, belong to someone else.

She has been here for twenty four hours. The queue has not moved since she joined it at two thirty AM and it is now five. She flew in from San Francisco, from Vegas. She has to get home to Nairobi. Her sister died on Monday. She smiles and her eyes brim a little when she says it. She blinks it away and changes the subject.

Her grief is very different from the woman next to me on the plane from Scotland, a woman with a name as old as the country and a face as familiar as my mother's. Her husband died in a car

crash last year. She was in Yorkshire at the time, with a nine year
old nephew who had a brain tumour. She went to another funeral
last week as well and all her friends have cancer. Death stalks me
on this trip.

My pashmina'd friend and I pass the time complaining about
the queue. What are they doing up there? Is there someone there?
We complain on behalf of other people: there are women with
children here, people in wheelchairs waiting here, old people. We
are showing each other that we are good women, because good
women never complain on their own behalf.

We plot our revenge. She will *never* fly through Dubai International again. It's not the terminal's fault, I say, but I will never fly
Emirates airlines again.

I will.

Some arts administrator working for less than a student grant
or a small publishing house will buy my flights and I will not have
the heart to make them change it. There was a terrible storm over
Dubai, an act of God. No one is to blame.

She works for a health insurance business in Vegas and I ask
about the US health reforms. The conflict of loyalties shows in her
voice, she whispers to me that the health care is better in Kenya
than the US. When she had her daughter she stayed in hospital
for six days and they showed her how to do everything. Her girl-
friends in Vegas have to leave the next day because they can't
afford it. They all get depressed.

She has been here for twenty four hours but she is lucky
because her niece is a stewardess for this airline. She called her in
New York and got access to the Executive Service Suite. She slept

on a chair and had biscuits and juice. The queue wasn't here when she first came down. She should have waited.

The men in front shift their weight and I glimpse the front of the queue. Right in front of the desk, leaning ostentatiously on it, is a woman with dyed blonde hair. She is laughing to her friend. She is the only person in the queue who is smiling.

A tired, slight woman in a sari walks up to a small fork in the queue, looking anxiously down to the desk. She is carrying a little girl, asleep, almost as big as she is.

'I think we should get this lady to the front,' says my Nairobi-Vegas friend.

'Absolutely,' I say.

She doesn't do anything. Even as I step forward I know that this is the pattern of my life: every best friend I have ever had was prettier than me and every one of them was a passive agitator. I am a moral Golem. I wade out into the crowd, ready to incur the wrath of everyone. 'Excuse me?' I say to the lady with the child. 'Are you waiting alone?'

She nods.

'Excuse me.' I am a fool. 'Excuse me, sir?' I am a big fool, the queue is ugly and we are all angry. 'I wonder if the people in front would mind very much...' I am touching the elbows of strangers and making an achingly familiar mistake. This will end in a shouty confrontation, possibly in languages I don't understand. 'If you would mind very much if this lady went to the front of the queue since she has a child...'

'No,' says the lady softly, 'My husband...' She points to an unlikely man, older, strange ribbed jumper. He's looking back at us.

'Oh, I thought you were alone.'

'No, but thank you. My husband is…'

The husband looks at her, cross, as if she has reproached him. He waves her back to the seats. I slip back into my place. Every best friend I ever had smiles up at me and I know that I am every big, daft best friend she has ever had. I smile back.

The tall man with the Kenyan passport turns to us. He is wearing a brown suit and a pork pie hat and his skin is the colour of Bournville chocolate. 'Madam, you are very kind,' he says. I blush because I tried to be good but made a big show of it, which is worse than not even trying to be good. And because he is so handsome.

Angela from Vegas-Nairobi and I have recognised each other from everywhere and we are now very close friends. Her husband is a hydroengineer. She is used to living in Vegas now but it's not where she would choose. She likes Oregon and so do I. Angela and I like rain.

I keep her place as she goes to the bathroom to freshen up, and she does the same for me while I go to the loo for a wee.

While she is away I see a man's head bob in front of the smiling blonde. There is someone behind the desk. They aren't doing anything, but there is someone there. I tell everyone I saw him but they can't see him. Angela believes me.

A suspicion forms on our side of the room that queues on the other side are moving. Some people break away, leaving their places and go over to the other side. After a while they all filter back, retaking their previous places, unchallenged.

We have been in the queue for three hours. Some people look for alternatives to just waiting. They stop passing air hostesses in their distinctive uniforms and head scarves. How are we to get to where we are going? People state their cases, say why they deserve extra help: business meetings must be kept, family obligations must be met. The angry camp man will already miss his balloon ride over Brisbane. There's no point in going now. This holiday was not meant to be. Even in the run up to it he knew he should not have come. He wants someone to ask him about it. No one does.

We have been here for four hours. Her flight is due to leave in two and there are seven people in front of us. I'm so tired I find myself swaying on my feet. My legs ache. My calves are pink from standing. We will never leave this queue.

Angela met her husband in Nairobi. She shows me his photo on her phone, tagged 'Stud Muffin'. I'm a little disappointed in her.

She has five sisters and four brothers: her father kept trying for sons and getting girls. She is the youngest. Her sisters told her scary things about guys when she was young. Whoever she dated got a hard time coming to the house. We show each other phone photos and pretend to be interested in each other's children. Really, we are taking turns to talk about our own. We say how hard it is to be away, how they will be allowed to eat pizza every night and watch TV all day. But we are both glad they are not here with us, waiting.

The business class queue is moving. The man dealing with the queue stands on a box and calls over the crowd, 'Anymore in first or business class?' He won't help us, only First class and Business class. Angela shouts that it is not fair and I join in. We shout long after the man has left his post and slipped out of the side door. We shout that it is not fair, we have been waiting, boo! Boo to you! We're not even angry any more. It's just a bit of fun.

All around small groups have formed, unlikely groups. A very fat African American man and a tall white Afrikaner woman with no-nonsense-shoes are getting each other water and cake. The man makes a big thing of saying he never eats cake. He makes her eat it. Her phone rings while her mouth is full and she splutters that her battery is about to run out and she doesn't need a driver now, she will go straight to Bangladesh. She is cut off and tuts accusingly at her phone.

The fat American must get there soon. He cannot be delayed much longer.

Suddenly, 'Thank you *very* much.' It is the blonde woman at the front. She has been served. She has a boarding pass for a flight tucked into her passport, holds it high over her head as she works her way back through the tightly woven queue, she is grinning. Every eye in the room follows her documents. Excitement ripples through the room.

The door to behind the desks opens and an older man in a crumpled suit comes in. We hear the sound of tickets being printed and telephones on speaker phone, perpetually engaged. The older man argues with someone on the phone. The queue is moving.

Angela's sister was fifty six and died of an aneurism. She complained of a head ache and the next thing she fell into a coma. They operated and she started to respond to reflex tests. They thought she was coming back but the doctors missed another bleed into her brain. Angela says she suffocated. I don't understand the story but feel it would be rude to ask her to explain.

She asks what I do, and I don't lie like I usually do, don't say I'm a waitress or an academic: I tell her I write detective novels and comics. She likes Danielle Steel but will read one of my books and write me about it. Maybe she will come to Scotland with her family. Maybe I will come through Vegas on a tour and we will meet again. I am forty three and I know we won't meet again. But I also know we are both sincere when we say we would like to.

Angela gets a ticket for Nairobi. She has to run to catch her flight. We hug a warm, fond good bye and I lift her off her feet. I ask her sister's name and am dismayed to realise that even as I am saying it back I have forgotten it.

The Brisbane man's queue is moving fast. He overtakes me. As he leaves with his boarding pass he tells me that he is going to Brisbane after all. He can leave in a few hours and he is going to try to have a good time, make the best of it. I doubt him.

I am served by the surly helper, the helper who is no help at all, who has been here with us all this time, not intervening, not helping. He does not make eye contact. He looks tired and browbeaten.

I am absurdly grateful to him. I have only seven and half hours to wait for a new connection. Now I can ascend on the long escalator to the duty-free shops and go and sit and piss at will, I am free to drink hot coffee and eat not-Dundee-cake and almost buy an ornamental gift box of Double Happiness cigarettes thinking they are chocolates.

Thank you very, very much, I say, euphoric that the wait is over, not knowing that the exhausted man has sent my luggage to Mali.

RED WOLVES IN
THE MIST

by ELIZABETH LAIRD

T HE WOLF CAME towards us out of the mist, trotting on stilted legs. He was lean but his black-tipped tail was bushy. Unlike his grey European cousins, he was rust-red, bright enough to stand out vividly against the chalky green vegetation.

I'd cursed the cloud which had rolled down upon us as we'd driven up through the belt of juniper and eucalyptus forest which ringed the lower slopes of this high plateau in Ethiopia's Bale Mountain region. But the mist had begun to clear enough for our eyes to follow the wolf's jerky progress across the tree-less ground. He turned and looked at our Land Rover, weaving his head from side to side as if to focus his eyes. His snout was long. He opened his mouth to yawn and his slim tongue curled back into his mouth. Then he trotted on.

'He is a juvenile,' my companion, Tsegaye, said. 'His coat is not so red yet.'

We abandoned the car and set off on foot across the spongy ground, which was pitted with the burrows of mole rats, the wolves' chief source of food. I struggled to fill my lungs in the thin air and shivered in the biting wind. An eagle circled above us, calling mournfully. There was no other sound, except for the crunch of our feet on the tiny Afro-Alpine flowers, blue, yellow, white and purple, and the crackle of Tsegaye's cheap nylon anorak. I had never before been wrapped in such a silence.

We took shelter from the wind behind a cow-sized boulder. It was spattered with lichens: stiff, yellow-grey, coral-like growths, flat rosettes of burning orange and clumps of green moss. They looked like splashes of paint. Scrapings in the earth behind the rock showed where a wolf had begun to hollow out a den.

The mist was lifting properly now and some way below us, on the track where we had left the Land Rover, a caravan of pack ponies had appeared. The small chestnut horses wore crimson saddlecloths and were laden with white sacks of grain. They seemed out of place in this moon-like landscape.

'They are merchants,' said Tsegaye. 'That is the highest road in Africa.'

He pulled the collar of his anorak higher round his neck. His head was shaved up the sides to leave a mop of black curls on top. His skin was the warm red-brown of the Ethiopian highlander.

A dog ran behind the pack ponies. Tsegaye shook his head at the sight of it. The dog looked innocent enough but it represented a threat, I knew. There are fewer than five hundred of Ethiopia's red wolves in the entire world. They are scattered about in the highest mountain regions, small populations separated from each other by vast stretches of lowland. There are none in captivity. As the population of Ethiopia surges, shepherds seeking new pastures drive their flocks ever higher towards the fragile mountain tops, bringing their dogs with them. It is the dog-borne infections of rabies and distemper which principally threaten the wolves. An epidemic can wipe out a significant proportion of their entire number in a season.

There is no great animosity between villagers and wolves.

'The farmers appreciate the cleverness of the wolf to hunt the mole rats,' Tsegaye told me. 'They do not take lambs from them, as jackals do.'

Not a curl of mist now remained and I could see the sweep of the plateau rising to even higher mountains beyond. Giant lobelias, palm-like plants, stood above the woody shrubs like single sentinels.

As we walked back to the Land Rover, mole rats bounced away from us, the fur on their fat brown rumps fluffed against the cold.

We saw three more wolves that morning. I bragged of this to Dr Karen Laurenson, one of the vets working on the wolf conservation project, when, shaking drops of moisture from our hair, we arrived back at the research station.

The scientists' house was a long building with a covered veranda on a steep hillside. Inside the fieldwork room, maps and charts were pinned to the bare wooden walls, and a table was littered with lab equipment, old notebooks, abstracts of theses, a tilly lamp and a vase of scarlet flowers.

The scientists running the project were dauntingly energetic. Enduring the cold, the monotony, the lack of comfort and the simplest diet, they were focussed entirely on the wolves. Here in the research station was evidence of the work: the education programme in the surrounding villages, charts recording dog inoculations, the birth of wolf pups and incidences of disease.

'Good luck today,' Karen announced, as we sat around in the glow of a lamp over a meal of spaghetti. 'Eve's found a dead horse.'

'Well, it was dying so I hastened its end.' Eve Pleydell, blonde and pretty, was delicately winding spaghetti round her fork. 'I thought it would come in handy.'

'Do you want to come out with us tonight?' Karen asked me. 'We're going to use the horse as bait and see if we can dart some hyenas. We need to know if they're a reservoir for rabies and canine distemper, like the dogs. We'll have a go at testing them for antibodies.'

We found the horse conveniently positioned on a grazing place where hyenas often came at night, not far from a small town. The pick-up bumped over the rough ground until its headlamps lit the dark lump of the dead creature lying on the ground. A small group of people were clustered round it. Eve had set a man to guard it, and others had come out to see what was going on.

Tsegaye and Idris, another worker on the project, shone their torches on the corpse. It was a horrible sight, its belly already swollen, its old sores scabrous, its hide patchy with mange, its tongue falling out, its dead protruding eye white and glazed. Karen and Eve picked up a hind leg each and flipped the thing over.

'Anyone got a machete?' Karen asked. 'We'd better chop off some pieces.'

Eve produced her penknife, slit the skin by the hip joint and stuck her fingers into the bloody mess. The watching men, wrapped up against the biting cold in their shroud-like white shawls, made loud remarks which, perhaps fortunately, neither young woman could understand.

'Okay. Let's pull the leg off now,' said Eve, grabbing it and twisting it round. There was a sound of tearing flesh and she staggered back with the leg in her hands. Karen had fished out the horse's liver and baited it with anaesthetic. She now stuffed it back into the horse's body.

'Idris, could you ask these people to go away?' she said. 'Any minute now, they're going to be surrounded by hyenas.'

There should have been a full moon but clouds were covering the sky. From the small town I could hear the thump, thump of a generator. Dogs barked and a lorry revved its engine.

I helped Eve to set a loudspeaker on the roof while Karen loaded the fearsome-looking dart-gun. Only a few flickers of light from the houses in the town pierced the darkness. I could see a faint outline of hills, rising and dipping on the horizon against a pale edging of sky which was lit dimly by the moon behind the clouds.

Karen and Eve worked steadily, preparing their equipment, head torches strapped on. It was the first time they had tried doing this, and they had planned it meticulously.

'If we get a hyena down, we're doing the measuring and the whole works, right?' Eve asked Karen.

'Yes.'

The loudspeakers were now ready on the roof.

'I'll just load up two darts,' said Karen, pushing a syringe into the anaesthetic phial. 'Idris, did you ask those guys? It's getting a bit crowded round here.'

Idris clearly knew the men well and was a skilled go-between. He talked to them quietly, answering questions, keeping his body language respectful, and after some laughter and murmurs of agreement his good manners worked and the onlookers moved off into the darkness.

'Get in the back of the car,' said Karen to me. 'If you're outside the hyenas won't come anywhere near.'

She backed the pick-up away, leaned the dart-gun on the open window, and pointed it towards the dead horse. Eve sat beside her. I was squashed between Idris and Tsegaye, grateful not only for the warmth of their bodies, as it was now very cold, but also for their reassuring bulk which separated me from the darkness outside, which now felt full of menace. Eve flicked a switch on the tape recorder connected to the loudspeaker on the roof and the air was filled with the bellow of an animal in the extremity of suffering.

'A dying wildebeest. I got it from the Serengeti,' Karen said.

And now, over this unearthly, gut-wrenching wail, I could hear the whooping calls of hyenas. I tried to suppress my shudder, not wanting to betray myself to the men beside me.

The moon came out. I could make out the shape of the dead horse but nothing else.

'Hey! What's that?' said Eve.

'Damn! A dog. The hyenas'll keep away if there are dogs around.'

Idris bravely got out of the pick-up and made rushes at the dog, trying to scare it, but it dodged past him, grabbed the baited liver out of the horse's body and ran off.

'It'll take him a while to sleep that off,' said Karen. 'Must be another dead horse somewhere around. By now you'd have expected a dozen hyenas, right in close. We'll have to move Dobbin further out of town.'

She reversed the pick-up back towards the horse and Eve tied the tow-rope round one of its remaining legs. We bumped away across the grazing land on which the grass had been shaved by cows' teeth down to a thin velvet, with the ghastly remains of the horse bouncing along behind us, and stopped again to begin another long wait.

The moon was fully out now. We sat in silence in the Land Rover hearing nothing but the groaning of the wildebeest from the roof and the occasional shriek of a nightbird. I felt the presence of the mangled horse, its throat cut, waiting for the final horror to begin. Straining our ears, we heard at last the derisive howls of hyenas from close by. They were circling us and we could sense their nervousness and doubt. They were too far away to shoot at.

'They're scared,' Karen said at last. 'They don't like the car and the smell of people. Let's give it up for tonight.'

'I'll take another leg off the horse,' said Eve. 'We can always find a use for it.'

I couldn't help feeling relieved. I had been safely cocooned between two beefy Ethiopians in the back of a large vehicle. There had been no danger to me, but a primitive horror had made my hair stand on end. I had some small inkling of what it must be like to live in a flimsy house, the walls made of nothing stouter than flimsy sticks or matting with a door of simple wooden planks, while outside in the dark powerful creatures prowl, waiting for a chance to tear me to pieces.

It's ten years now since I watched the wolves on their mountain tops and saw the conservation team at work. Since then, not much has changed. Rabies has struck again, twice, but the wolves have clung on, bringing themselves back once more from the brink and producing sturdy litters year by year.

I wrote a novel for children about the wolves of Ethiopia. It was called *Red Wolf*, and soon went out of print. But I think often of those lean, elegant creatures and the brave people trying to hold at bay the dangers that threaten to overwhelm them. From the heat and hassle of London, their cold, remote world seems unbearably beautiful: a precious, fragile place. The wolves pass their days as they always have done, pursuing their plump little victims, courting each other, giving birth and caring for their young. Tiny bright flowers are their carpet. Swirling clouds hide and then reveal them.

We are all implicated in the wolves' plight. In a feeble shake of my fist at the forces of planetary destruction, I plant up my garden with vegetables and put out my newspapers to be recycled. Nothing I do will be enough.

I want the wolves to survive. I want their world to survive.

THE SAGA OF
RAGNAR ERIKSON

by MICHAEL MORPURGO

14ᵗʰ July 1965.

As I SAILED into Arnefjord this morning, I was looking all around me, marvelling at the towering mountains, at the still dark waters, at the welcoming escort of porpoises, at the chattering oyster-catchers, and I could not understand for the life of me why the Vikings ever left this land.

It was beautiful beyond belief. Why would you ever leave this paradise of a place, to face the heaving grey of the Norwegian Sea, and a voyage into the unknown, when you had all this outside your door?

The little village at the end of the fjord looked at first too good to be true – a cluster of clapboard houses gathered around the quay, most painted ox-blood red. On top of the hill beyond them stood a simple wooden church with an elegant pencil-sharp spire, and a well-tended graveyard, surrounded by a white picket fence. There seemed to be flowers on almost every grave. A stocky little Viking pony grazed the meadow below.

The fishing boat tied up at the quay had clearly seen better days. Now that I was closer, I noticed that the village too wasn't as well kept as I had first thought. In places the paint was peeling off the houses. There were tiles missing from the rooftops, and a few of the windows were boarded up. It wasn't abandoned, but the whole place looked tired, and sad somehow.

As I came in on the motor there was something about the village that began to make me feel uncomfortable. There was no one to be seen, not a soul. Only the horse. No smoke rose from the chimneys. There was no washing hanging out. No one was fishing from the shoreline, no children played in the street or around the houses.

I hailed the boat, hoping someone might be on board to tell me where I could tie up. There was no reply. So I tied up on the quay anyway and jumped out. I was looking for a café, somewhere I could get a drink, or even a hot meal. And I needed a shop too. I was low on water, and I had no beer left on board, and no coffee.

I found a place almost immediately that looked as if it might be the village stores. I peered through the window. Tables and chairs were set out. There was a bar to one side, and across the room I could see a small shop, the shelves stacked with tins. Things were looking up, I thought. But I couldn't see anyone inside. I tried the door, and to my surprise it opened.

I'd never seen anything like it. This was shop, café, nightclub, post office, all in one. There was a Wurlitzer juke box in the corner, and then to one side, opposite the bar, the post office and shop. And there was a piano right next to the post office counter, with sheet music open on the top – Beethoven Sonatas.

I called out, but still no one emerged. So I went outside again and walked down the village street, up the hill towards the church, stopping on the way to stroke the horse. I asked him if he was alone here, but he clearly thought that this was a stupid question and wandered off, whisking his tail as he went.

The church door was open, so I went in and sat down, breathing in the peace of the place, and trying at the same time to suppress the thought that this might be some kind of ghost village. It was absurd, I knew it was, but I could feel the fear rising inside me.

That was when the bell rang loud, right above my head, from the spire. Twelve times. My heart pounded in my ears. As the last echoes died away I could hear the sound of a man coughing and muttering to himself. It seemed to come from high up in the gallery behind me. I turned.

We stood looking at one another, not speaking for some time. I had the impression he was as surprised to see me as I was to see him. He made his way down the stairs, and came slowly up the aisle towards me.

He had strange eyes this man, unusually light, like his hair. He might have been fifty or sixty, but weathered, like the village was.

'Looking at you,' he began, 'I would say you might be English.'

'You'd be right,' I told him.

'Thought so,' he said, nodding. Then he went on, 'I ring the bell every day at noon. I always have. It's to call them back. They will come one day. You will see, they will come.'

I didn't like to ask who he was talking about. My first thought was that perhaps he was a little mad.

'You need some place to stay, young man? I have twelve houses you can choose from. You need to pray? I have a church. You need something to eat, something to drink? I have that too. Yes, you're looking a little pale. I can tell you need a drink. Come.'

Outside the church he stopped to shake my hand and to introduce himself as Ragnar Erikson. As we walked down the hill he told me who lived in each of the houses we passed – a cousin here, an aunt there – and who grew the best vegetables in the village, and who was the best pianist. He spoke as if they were still there, and this was all very strange because it was quite obvious to me by now that no one at all was living in any of these houses. Then I saw he was leading me back to where I'd been before, into the bar-cum-post office-cum-village stores.

'You want some music on the Wurlitzer?' he asked me. 'Help yourself, whatever you like, *A Whiter Shade of Pale*, *Sloop John B*, *Rock Around the Clock*. You choose. It's free, no coins needed.'

I chose *A Whiter Shade of Pale*, while he went behind the bar and poured me a beer.

'I don't get many people coming here these days,' he said. 'And there's only me living here now, so I don't keep much in the bar or the shop. But I caught a small salmon today. We shall have that for supper, and a little schnapps. You will stay for supper, won't you? You must forgive me – I talk a lot, to myself mostly, so when I have someone else to talk to, I make up for lost talking time. You're the first person I've had in here for a month at least.'

I didn't know what to say. Too much was contradictory and strange. I longed to ask him why the place looked so empty and if there were people really living in those houses. And who was he ringing the church bell for? Nothing made any sense. But I couldn't bring myself to ask. Instead, I made polite conversation.

'You speak good English,' I told him.

'This is because Father and I, we went a lot to Shetland in the old days. So we had to speak English. We were always going over there.'

'In that fishing boat down by the quay?' I asked him.

'It is not a fishing boat,' he said. 'It is a supply boat. I carry supplies to the villages up and down the fjords. There is no road, you see; everything has to come by boat, the post as well. So I am the postman too.'

After a couple of beers he took me outside and back down to the quayside to show me his boat. Once on board, I could see it was the kind of boat that no storm could sink. It was made not for speed but for endurance, built to bob up and down like a cork and just keep going. The boat suited the man, I thought. We stood together in the wheelhouse, and I knew he wanted to talk.

'My family,' he said, 'we had two boats, this one and one other just the same. Father made one, I made the other. This is the old boat, my father's boat. He made it with his own hands before I was born, and we took it over to Shetland, like the Vikings did before us. But we were not on a raid like they were. It was during the wartime, when the Germans were occupying Norway.

'We were taking refugees across the Norwegian Sea to Shetland, often twenty of them at a time, hidden down below. Sometimes they were Jews escaping from the Nazis. Sometimes it was airmen who had been shot down, commandos we had been hiding, secret agents too. Fifteen times we went there and back and they didn't catch us. Lucky, we were very lucky. This is a lucky boat. The other one, the one I built, was not so lucky.'

Ragnar Erikson wasn't the kind of man you could question or interrupt, but I was wondering all through our supper of herring and salmon, in the warmth of his kitchen that evening, what he had meant about the other boat. And I still hadn't dared to broach the subject that puzzled me most: why there seemed to be no one else living in the village. When he fell silent I felt he wanted to be lost in his thoughts, and so the right moment never came. But after supper by the fire, he began to question me closely about why I had come sailing to Norway, about what I was doing with my life. He was easy to talk to because he seemed genuinely interested. So I found myself telling him everything: how at thirty-one I had found myself alone in the world, that my mother had died when I was a child, and just a couple of months ago my father had too. I was a schoolteacher, but not at all sure I wanted to go on being one.

'But why did you come here?' he asked me. 'Why Norway?'

So I told him how, when I was a boy, I had been obsessed by the Vikings; I'd loved the epic stories of Beowulf and Grendel; I'd even learned to read the runes. It had become a lifelong ambition of mine to come to Norway one day. But arriving here in this particular fjord had been an accident – I was just looking for a good sheltered place to tie up for the night.

'I'm glad you came,' he said after a while. 'As I said, no one comes here much these days. But they will, they will.'

'Who will?' I asked him, without thinking, and at once regretted it for I could see he was frowning at me, looking at me quite hard suddenly, and I feared I might have offended him.

'Whoever it is, they will be my family and my friends, that's all I know,' he said. 'They will live in the houses, where they all once lived, where their souls still live.'

I could hear from the tone of his voice that there was more to tell and that he might tell it, if I was patient and did not press him. So I kept quiet, and waited. I'm so pleased I did. When at last he began again he told me the whole story, about the empty village, about the other boat, the boat he talked about as if it had been cursed.

'I think perhaps you would like to know why I'm all alone in this place?' he said, looking directly at me. It felt as if he was having to screw up all his courage before he could go on.

'I should have gone to the wedding myself,' he said, 'with everyone else in the village, but I did not want to. It was only in Flam, down the fjord just north of here, not that far. The thing was, that ever since I was a little boy, the bride had been my sweetheart, the love of my life, but I was always too timid to tell her. I looked for her every time I went to Flam to collect supplies, met her whenever I could, went swimming with her, picking berries, mountain climbing, but I never told her how I felt. Now she was marrying someone else. I didn't want to be there, that's all. So my father skippered my boat that day instead of me. There were fourteen people in the boat – everyone from the village except for me and two very old spinster sisters. They did everything together, those two. One of them was too sick to go, so the other insisted on staying behind to look after her. I watched the boat going off into the morning mists. I never saw it again, nor anyone on board.

'To this day, no one really knows what happened. But we do know that early in the evening, after the wedding was over, there was a rock-slide, a huge avalanche which swept down the mountainside into the fjord, and set up a great tidal wave. People from miles around heard it and saw it. No one saw the boat go down, but that's what must have happened.

'For a few years the two old sisters and I kept the village going. When they died, within days of one another, I buried them in the churchyard. Then I was alone. To start with, very often, I thought of leaving, but someone had to tend the graves, had to ring the church bell, so I stayed. I fished, I kept a few sheep in those days. I had my horse. I learned how to be alone.

'I discovered there is one thing you have to do when you are alone, and that is to keep busy. So every day I work on the houses, opening windows in the summers to air rooms, lighting fires in the winters to warm them through, painting windows and doors, fixing where I can, just keeping them ready for the day they return.

There's always something. I know it's looking more and more untidy as the years go by, but I do my best. I have to. They're all living here still, all my family and friends. I can feel them all about me. They're waiting, and I'm waiting, for the others to come and join them.'

'I don't understand,' I told him.

'No, young man,' he said, laughing a little. 'I'm not off my head, not quite. I know the dead cannot come back. But I do know their spirits live on, and I do know that one day, if I do not leave, if I keep ringing the bell, if I keep the houses dry, then people will find this place, will come and live here. In the villages nearby, they are still frightened of the place. They think it is cursed somehow. But they are wrong about that. It was the boat that was cursed, I tell them, not the village. Anyway, they do not come. Most of them are so frightened, they won't even come to visit me. They say it is a dying village and will soon be a dead village. But it is not, and it will not be, not so long as I stay. One day people will come and then the village will be alive once more. I know this for sure.'

Ragnar Erikson offered me a bed in his house that night, but I said I was fine in the boat. I am ashamed to admit it but after hearing his story I just didn't want to stay there any longer. It was too easy to believe that the place – paradise that it looked – might be cursed. He did not try to persuade me. I am sure he knew instinctively what I was feeling. I told him that I had to be up early in the morning, thinking I might not see him again. But

he said he would be sure to see me off. And he was as good as his word. He was down on the quay at first light. We shook hands warmly, friends for less than a day, but I felt, because he had told me his story, that in a way we were friends for life. He told me to come back one day and see him again if ever I was passing. Although I said I would, I knew how unlikely it would be. But, through all the things that have happened to me since, I never forgot the saga of Ragnar Erikson. It was a story that I liked to tell often to my family, to my friends.

1ˢᵗ August 2010. Midnight.

Today I came back to Arnefjord. It has been over forty years and I've often dreamed about it, wondering what happened to Ragnar Erikson and his dying village. This time I have brought my family, my grandchildren too, because however often I tell them the story, they never quite seem to believe it.

I had my binoculars out at the mouth of the little fjord and saw the village at once. It was just as it had been. Even the boat was there at the quay, with no one on it, so far as I could see. There was no smoke rising from the chimneys; when we tied up, no one came to see us. I walked up towards the village shop, the grand-children running off into the village, happy to be ashore, skipping about like goats, finding their land legs again.

Then, as I walked up towards the church, I saw a mother coming towards me with a pushchair.

'Do you live here?' I asked her.

'Yes,' she said, and pointed out her house, 'over there.'

My granddaughter came running up to me.

'I knew it, Grandpa,' she cried, 'I always knew it was just a story. Of course there are people living here. I've seen lots and lots of them.'

And she was right. There was a toy tractor outside the back door of a newly painted house, and I could hear the sound of shrieking children coming from further away down by the seashore.

'What story does she mean?' the mother asked me.

So I told her how I'd come here over forty years before and had met Ragnar Erikson, and how he was the only one living here then.

'Old Ragnar,' she said, smiling. 'He's up in the churchyard now.'

She must have seen the look on my face. 'No, no,' she said, 'I don't mean that. He's not dead. He's doing the flowers. We wouldn't be here if it wasn't for him. Ragnar saved this village, Ragnar and the road.'

'The road?' I asked.

'Fifteen years ago they built a road to the village, and suddenly it was a place people could come to and live in. But there would have been no village if Ragnar hadn't stayed, we all know that. There are sixteen of us living here – six families. He's old now and does not hear so well, but he is strong enough to walk up the hill to ring the bell. It was the bell that brought us back, he says. And he still likes to go on ringing it every day. Habit, he says.'

I went up the hill with my granddaughter, who ran on ahead of me up the steps and into the church. When she came out there was an old man with her, and he was holding her hand.

'She has told me who you are,' he said. 'But I would have recognised you anyway. I knew you would come back, you know. You must have heard me ringing. If I remember rightly, you liked *Whiter Shade of Pale* on the Wurlitzer. And you liked a beer. Do you remember?'

'I remember,' I said. 'I remember everything.'

THE BALLAD OF JEMMY BUTTON

by JULIA DONALDSON

Around Cape Horn the wind howls cold; the glaciers meet the sea.
A captain came with button box to bid for natives three.

He named the man York Minster; Fuegia Basket was the maid.
The boy was Jemmy Button, which is how his price was paid.

York Minster was a moody man, Fuegia small and shy,
And sixteen-year-old Jemmy had a twinkle in his eye.

'You shall not paint your faces red or grease your copper skins,
Use porpoise jaws to comb your hair or shells to shave your
    chins.

You shall not feed on penguin meat, on dolphins or on seals
But you shall eat boiled mutton and say grace before your meals.

In England you shall spend a year, and then sail home again
To turn your savage brothers into Christian gentlemen.'

He took them back to England and he carried out his plan.
They learnt that God made Adam and that manners makyth man.

Fuegia Basket learnt to sew; she mended York's cravats
And stitched the shiny buttons on to Jemmy Button's spats.

And when the year was over and they sailed again to sea
The ship was full of gravy-boats and tablecloths and tea.

At last they reached their homeland and they rowed their boats
    upstream.
The natives gathered round to gaze at figures from a dream.

But Jemmy's sisters scattered when they saw him in his spats.
His brothers circled him like dogs and stared at him like cats.

He spoke to them in English but they did not understand,
And Jemmy could no longer speak the language of his land.

The crew put up three wigwams and they dug three garden plots,
Then sailed away and left them with their china chamberpots.

The natives went for Jemmy and they trampled on his beans.
York Minster and Fuegia Basket stole his soup tureens.

When next the captain called he found young Jemmy Button thin.
His hair was coarse, his eyes were dim, he wore an otter skin.

'Come back, young Jemmy Button, come and sail across the sea.
Oh leave the howling glaciers and come back home with me.'

'Oh no,' says Jemmy Button, 'I shall never leave Cape Horn,
But stay and hunt for otters in the land where I was born.'

The Elsewhere collection was commissioned by the Edinburgh International Book Festival, thanks to a generous grant from Creative Scotland and the Scottish Government's Edinburgh Festivals Expo Fund. In an innovative publishing and design partnership, Glasgow-based publisher Cargo and San Francisco-based publisher McSweeney's have produced the Elsewhere box set of four themed volumes.

EDINBURGH INTERNATIONAL BOOK FESTIVAL
Commissioning editors: Nick Barley, Sara Grady, Roland Gulliver
Copy editors: Jennifer Richards, Oisín Murphy-Lawless
Thanks to: Amanda Barry, Andrew Coulton, Elizabeth Dunlop,
Helen Moffat, Nicola Robson, Kate Seiler, Janet Smyth

edbookfest.co.uk

CARGO
Publishing director: Mark Buckland
Managing editor: Helen Sedgwick
Thanks to: Alistair Braidwood, Martin Brown, Rodge Glass,
Brian Hamill, Craig Lamont, Anneliese Mackintosh, Gill Tasker

cargopublishing.com

McSWEENEY'S
Design and art direction: Brian McMullen,
Adam Krefman, Walter Green
Illustrations: Jack Teagle
Thanks to: all at McSweeney's

mcsweeneys.net